René Lévesque, 1922-1987

Marguerite Paulin

Marguerite Paulin is host and producer of a radio program in Montreal on which she interviews writers. She holds a doctorate, has been a lecturer for ten years at McGill University, and has also taught CEGEP. She has published fiction and essays and has written three other biographies for XYZ's "Les grandes figures" series: *Félix Leclerc, Louis-Joseph Papineau*, and *Maurice Duplessis*.

The translator: Jonathan Kaplansky

Jonathan Kaplansky works as a literary translator in Ottawa; he completed Master's degrees in Translation at the University of Ottawa and in French Language and Literature at McGill. He has translated work by Hélène Rioux, Robert Dickson, Sylvie Massicotte, and Hervé Dumont and also translated the biography *Samuel de Champlain: Father of New France* for the Quest Library series.

In the same collection .

Ven Begamudré, *Isaac Brock: Larger Than Life*.
Lynne Bowen, *Robert Dunsmuir: Laird of the Mines*.
Kate Braid, *Emily Carr: Rebel Artist*.
Kathryn Bridge, *Phyllis Munday: Mountaineer*.
William Chalmers, *George Mercer Dawson: Geologist, Scientist, Explorer*.
Judith Fitzgerald, *Marshall McLuhan: Wise Guy*.
lian goodall, *William Lyon Mackenzie King: Dreams and Shadows*.
Stephen Eaton Hume, *Frederick Banting: Hero, Healer, Artist*.
Naïm Kattan, *A.M. Klein: Poet and Prophet*.
Betty Keller, *Pauline Johnson: First Aboriginal Voice of Canada*.
Michelle Labrèche-Larouche, *Emma Albani: International Star*.
Wayne Larsen, *A.Y. Jackson: A Love for the Land*.
Francine Legaré, *Samuel de Champlain: Father of New France*.
Margaret Macpherson, *Nellie McClung: Voice for the Voiceless*.
Dave Margoshes, *Tommy Douglas: Building the New Society*.
Raymond Plante, *Jacques Plante: Behind the Mask*.
T.F. Rigelhof, *George Grant: Redefining Canada*.
Arthur Slade, *John Diefenbaker: An Appointment with Destiny*.
Roderick Stewart, *Wilfrid Laurier: A Pledge for Canada*.
John Wilson, *John Franklin: Traveller on Undiscovered Seas*.
John Wilson, *Norman Bethune: A Life of Passionate Conviction*.
Rachel Wyatt, *Agnes Macphail: Champion of the Underdog*.

René Lévesque

National Library of Canada Cataloguing in Publication

Paulin, Marguerite, 1955-

    René Lévesque : charismatic leader

    (The Quest library ; 23)
    Translation of: René Lévesque : une vie, une nation.
    Includes bibliographical references and index.
    ISBN 1-894852-13-3

    1. Lévesque, René, 1922-1987. 2. Québec (Province) – History – Autonomy and independence movements. 3. Parti québécois. 4. Québec (Province) – Politics and goverment – 1976-1985. 5. Prime ministers – Québec (Province) – Biography. 6. Journalists – Québec (Province) – Biography. I. Title. II. Series: Quest library ; 23.

FC2925.1.L5P3813 2004   971.4'04'092   C2004-941416-X

Legal Deposit: Fourth quarter 2004
National Library of Canada
Bibliothèque nationale du Québec

XYZ Publishing acknowledges the support of The Quest Library project by the Canadian Studies Program and the Book Publishing Industry Development Program (BPIDP) of the Department of Canadian Heritage. The opinions expressed do not necessarily reflect the views of the Government of Canada.

The publishers further acknowledge the financial support our publishing program receives from The Canada Council for the Arts, the ministère de la Culture et des Communications du Québec, and the Société de développement des entreprises culturelles.

Chronology: Michèle Vanasse
Index: Darcy Dunton
Layout: Édiscript enr.
Cover design: Zirval Design
Cover illustration: Francine Auger
Photo research: Michèle Vanasse

Printed and bound in Canada

XYZ Publishing
1781 Saint Hubert Street
Montreal, Quebec H2L 3Z1
Tel: (514) 525-2170
Fax: (514) 525-7537
E-mail: info@xyzedit.qc.ca
Web site: www.xyzedit.qc.ca

Distributed by: Fitzhenry & Whiteside
195 Allstate Parkway
Markham, ON L3R 4T8
Customer Service, tel: (905) 477-9700
Toll free ordering, tel: 1-800-387-9776
Fax: 1-800-260-9777
E-mail: bookinfo@fitzhenry.ca

International Rights: André Vanasse, tel. (514) 525-2170 # 25
E-mail: andre.vanasse@xyzedit.qc.ca

Lévesque
René

THE QUEST LIBRARY

CHARISMATIC LEADER

XYZ
Publishing

By the same author

Félix Leclerc: Filou, le toubadour. Montreal: XYZ, "Les grandes figures" series, 1998.
Louis-Joseph Papineau: Le grand tribun, le pacifiste. Montreal: XYZ, "Les grandes figures" series, 2000.
Maurice Duplessis. Le Noblet, le petit roi. Montreal: XYZ, "Les grandes figures" series, 2002.

For Mother,
for Alexis, my nephew,
for Iain Davidson

Thanks to:
André Vanasse
Michèle Vanasse
Xavier Gélinas

Since I've been working alongside him, René Lévesque appears to me to understand and feel deeply the contradictions of the Quebecer, at once compelled to break free and yet prevented from doing so. That's why he vacillates between darkness and light, impatience and confidence, tenderness and harshness, the middle ground and the extreme, in conversation with himself or with others.

CAMILLE LAURIN

Contents

1 I Don't Want to Destroy Canada   1
2 The Real Quiet Revolution   13
3 The Son of Maître Lévesque, Esquire   27
4 Seeing the War First Hand   37
5 A Passion for Communicating   45
6 Minister in the Lesage Government   57
7 Breaking Through the Wall of Fear   73
8 The Moment of Truth   91
9 "… an old tree forgotten in the plains"   107

Chronology of
René Lévesque
(1922-1987)   125
Bibliography   147

René Lévesque at a press conference at a construction site in Longueuil in 1981.

1

I Don't Want to Destroy Canada

"**M**y dear friends, if I have understood you well…" René Lévesque attempts to silence his supporters gathered together at the Paul Sauvé Centre. Two women stand behind him, in the background: Corinne Côté, his wife, and Lise Payette, Minister Responsible for the Status of Women and the only cabinet member present at this occasion. Wearing black, as if symbolically in mourning.

From the bleachers to the floor, signs reading "oui" alternate with Fleur-de-lis flags. In the distance, a few voices strike up "Mon cher René, c'est à ton tour," and spontaneously thousands of supporters join in the Gilles Vigneault song to pay homage to their leader's courage. Lévesque smiles sadly.

At a little before eight o'clock on May 20, 1980, the referendum results are official: 59.6 per cent of Quebecers have said "no." Some two million Quebecers refuse to give the government a mandate to negotiate a new political accord with the federal government.

It is a bitter defeat: over half the population has just rejected sovereignty-association. The leader of the Parti Québécois (PQ) assesses the extent of his power: before him, impassioned men and women await but one word to invade the streets of Montreal. One sign and they would force open the doors of the arena to show their sadness and disappointment.

René Lévesque had rewritten his speech several times. A democrat, the sovereigntist leader accepts the voters' decision. Now they have to live together, despite the fact that voters are divided. They must make peace with their opponents, with those who believe in federalism. The Parti Québécois leader again asks for silence. His voice rises above the shouting crowd:

"My dear friends... If I've understood you clearly, you've just said "Till the next time..."

The supporters roar their approval: they want to resume the struggle as soon as possible. The battle has been lost, but not the war.

Lévesque then spontaneously invites those present in the room to join in the "the most beautiful of Quebec songs." And, slightly off key, he strikes up "Gens du pays," the song the crowd had begun to sing earlier. The time for sadness has passed: solidarity has overridden rancour and bitterness. Leader of the PQ government since November 15, 1976, René Lévesque is, first and foremost, premier of all Quebecers. After four years in power, he is thinking of the next provincial election he must soon call.

René Lévesque wants to bring opposing forces together, and he is the man for the job.

∞

The referendum campaign had started long before it was officially called in March 1980.

Three years earlier, shortly after coming into power, René Lévesque had taken on a new responsibility: governing within Canadian Confederation while promoting the Parti Québécois' sovereigntist option.

"It all would have been simpler if a vote for us had meant a vote for independence," he regretted.

It was Claude Morin who proposed gradualism in 1972: win the election and then hold a referendum on Quebec sovereignty. "After all," he claimed, "the time is ripe for negotiation and consensus. The international community will never recognize our political status if we only scrape by to win."

René Lévesque also believed it necessary to consult the people before changing the country's constitution. At the November 1974 convention of the Parti Québécois, the referendum passed two to one. From then on, they aimed for the majority of the National Assembly. But members were divided. Lévesque had to exert influence so that the resolution could pass, which displeased some, certain of whom even tore up their membership cards.

"It was the first crisis that had the potential to completely ruin us," Lévesque confessed.

∞

After the Parti Québécois was elected on November 15, 1976, René Lévesque returned to the very essence of the Sovereignty-Association Movement that he had founded nine years earlier. "Today," he said, "I value this union more than ever!" It was a point of honour he set for himself. A sovereign Quebec must establish an economic partnership with Canada. On the strength of this faith, he curtailed the radical wing of the Parti Québécois that wanted to declare immediate independence. Lévesque was wary of idealists who didn't accept the ground rules of democracy.

"They're nitpicking troublemakers!" he said. "With left-wingers like these we'll rot from within."

From early 1977 on, the leader of the PQ needed to contain the aftershock. Lévesque had a heavy load to carry. One false move could endanger the entire party.

Any discussion among the party members – the Péquistes – inevitably resulted in a debate about the party's options. Should they hold the referendum in the first year of the mandate? No. The leader's response was unequivocal. Lévesque had other projects near to his heart, including passing a law on political party financing.

"There will be no more secret funds. Enough of giving money to friends of the party. I want the first law my government passes to give voters confidence."

Certain people advised him that he was taking a risk by putting the referendum on hold. Lévesque remained firm:

"As Claude Morin says, you can't force a flower to grow. Everything in good time."

"If we lose, we can expect criticism."

"And if we win," he added confidently, "people will say we had intuition."

∞

It was difficult to choose ministers among the seventy-one PQ members elected November 15. Lévesque would make some jealous and he warned those most in a hurry: his nominations were not cast in stone. In the Eastern Townships, where he had gone to escape for a few days, he said he would begin the never-ending task that was choosing a cabinet.

First, a list of the most likely names: Jacques Parizeau for Finance. What about Jacques-Yvan Morin for Culture? He tore up the piece of paper and began again. Then he remembered Robert Bourassa's advice. While playing at designating future PQ ministers, the Liberal leader had noted, "Monsieur Lévesque, you would be better off having so-and-so in your cabinet rather than outside it." He was right. The PQ leader worked on tirelessly, then went back to square one, determined this time to get it right.

∞

During his sixteen years in politics, René Lévesque had known ups and downs. In September, for example, he had considered throwing in the towel. But Claude Charron's interview in *Le Devoir* had galvanized him.

Being called a "little old man" and "dead wood" at age fifty-four was hard to swallow! Should he resign, make way for new blood? No! Retiring was out of the question. The Parti Québécois had to remain true to the commitments it had made at the last convention. Swinging too radically to the left was out of the question. The "little old man" was resilient. He ordered the discontented: "Leave! Go found your own party!" Everything could have fallen apart at that point. But luck had it that Robert Bourassa, banking on the excitement of the Olympics, prematurely called the election for November 15.

∞

His list completed, Lévesque met with each new minister. Jacques Parizeau was awarded the "triple crown": Minister of Finance, President of the Treasury Board, and Minister of Revenue. He thus held the most important position in the PQ cabinet. Jean Garon, named Minister of Agriculture, at first considered refusing. He was informed he would end up regretting it: Lévesque never forgot an insult and especially disliked being opposed. The PQ leader was soon to offer Claude Charron, who had openly opposed his leadership at the Handfield Inn, the Department of Youth and Sport – with the problem of the Olympic deficit as a bonus! This was a hot potato in the hands of the young rebel who had opposed the leader. And Lévesque named Lise Payette, who had hoped for Culture, as Minister of the Department of Consumer Affairs, Cooperatives, and Financial Institutions. Not very original, the only woman appointed to caucus told herself. A woman in the Liberal government had held the same position just before her!

"I didn't recruit people from the world of finance," René Lévesque proudly pointed out, emphasizing the contrast with economist Robert Bourassa's former Liberal government.

∽

Complex J building of the Grande-Allée in Quebec City was aptly called "the bunker." The elevator went right up to the cabinet room. Windowless, its walls covered in carpet, this softly lit strongroom looked like a flying saucer. Smack in the middle, an impressive horseshoe-shaped table dominated the entire room. "It looks like Dr. Strangelove's war room," remarked Lise Payette. "It feels as if we're isolated in a space capsule," added Lévesque. Before the opening of the first PQ Parliament, set for December 14, the meetings were like family get-togethers. People were becoming acquainted, sizing each other up. One, rather casual, removed his socks under the table; another grumbled constantly, contradicting everyone. All were on guard: they could not allow a colleague to eat into the slightest piece of their territory. It was a male chauvinist environment characterized by starchy ritual. On each side of the premier, in alphabetical order, alternating, the ministers sat properly in the seat designated by a card. The school of British parliamentarism was strict and disciplined. This first PQ cabinet was learning the ropes, and the students were well behaved. The most unruly waited until later before making themselves heard. René Lévesque had a moderating effect on the zealots: the people had voted against the Liberals, not for the PQ. Linguistic battles, the Olympic deficit, and the wear and tear of power had gotten the better of the Bourassa government. "We will try to learn from the errors of our predecessors." René Lévesque was especially fond of one project among several and kept returning to it: "We will give Quebecers a code of ethics in voting practices." Enough favouritism and insidious patronage. Any gift over twenty-five dollars had to be returned. Holding interest in companies doing business with the State was out of the question. People who had shares in the stock market had sixty days to dispose of them. Looking hard at each cabinet minister, Lévesque concluded:

"And if I ever catch one of you bribing anybody, I'll blow the whistle on you immediately!"

"Cancelling is out of the question. Yes, I'll be there." As planned, Lévesque went to the federal-provincial conference set before the election. "Deep down," he said to those close to him, "I want people to know that I do not want to destroy Canada. I am going to Ottawa in good faith, even though I think it's a waste of time." From the first day on, the Quebec delegation was questioned by journalists who hoped at every turn for confrontations between the separatist and the federalist. Lévesque versus Trudeau, the bitter rivals, as they liked to call them. For the prime minister of Canada, the PQ victory was practically a personal defeat. Now, making the best of things, he predicted the Péquiste government would not be able to hold on to power following the November 15 victory.

René Lévesque learned a tough lesson at this first meeting with his counterparts from other provinces. Against all expectations, seven provinces chose to penalize themselves by agreeing to two income tax points instead of four. To journalists seeking his impressions, Lévesque conceded that the inter-provincial alliance was a trap. "The others chose to let us down, even at the risk of losing millions from the federal government." Lévesque returned from Ottawa disappointed, convinced more than ever that sovereignty was the best solution for Quebec.

He set aside political quarrels and spoke of the upcoming vacation he would take with Corinne Côté. Yielding to his companion's insistent demands, he was going out openly with her.

"You're not afraid what people will say?" a friend asked him. "After all, you're still not divorced."

René Lévesque didn't worry about his reputation as a skirt chaser. He was uninfluenced by scruples, hated moralizing and worrying about gossip. Being premier would not change his attitude. He loved Corinne, whom he had met eight years earlier at the launch of his book *Option Québec* (*An Option for Quebec*). Among the guests jockeying for autographs, he had noticed a young Laval University student originally from Alma. Born into a Quebec nationalist family, Corinne Côté admired René Lévesque. He had left a well-established political party to begin a thrilling adventure, not knowing whether his courageous move held a future. Among the people congratulating him, Lévesque was entranced by the dark eyes of this woman twenty years his junior. The seducer was seduced. "Call me," he had written to her after seeing her again at a dinner with friends. What began as a fling, little by little developed into a love affair spanning nearly twenty years. He who had never let himself fall victim to love was now contemplating splitting up with his wife Louise. He would be the first Quebec head of state to divorce. And he didn't give a hoot about the gossip.

∞

To be witty or provoke people, René Lévesque considered himself a Yankeebécois. He liked the U.S., was fascinated by its history, its people, its geography. As soon as he had a chance, he would rush to the Atlantic coast where the ocean and scenery reminded him of his childhood in the Gaspé. Far from being a threat, he saw the United States as a democracy whose political institutions protected against excess. He admired the great dream of equality held by the founders of the American nation and personified by presidents such as Franklin Delano Roosevelt. FDR was his hero. The New Deal slogan, *We have nothing to fear but fear itself*, would serve as the point of departure for his sovereigntist manifesto *Option Québec*. For Lévesque, Europe was far away. On the other hand, America was on the same continent. For better or for worse. He was also thrilled, at the beginning of his mandate, to receive an invitation to give a talk to members of the

Economic Club of New York. Robert Bourassa had had to wait three years before being extended the same privilege! But Lévesque was not taken in by the honour: the Wall Street financiers seemed quite impatient to meet the leader of a party that wanted the separation of Quebec.

René Lévesque worked on his speech until late in the night, seeking the right idea, the words that would strike a chord with his hosts. He scratched out a sentence that he had left unfinished. No one else was allowed to look at his speech. When it came to explaining his ideas, he once more became the journalist of the program that had made him famous. René Lévesque forever remained the star of *Point de mire*.

Before leaving for New York, those accompanying him insisted on reading his speech. "We have to modify certain expressions, nuance things." When the premier heard of this order, he categorically refused to change so much as a comma. He refused to address the bankers of the Economic Club any differently from the way he had always addressed Quebec voters. On January 24, an airplane landed on a private field in New Jersey, with the Quebec delegation on board. The next day, the Quebec premier was to meet powerful America, the big boys on Wall Street. René Lévesque was nervous and impatient. He had to prove that his government was a credible player in the eyes of the most imposing empire in the world, to show that the Parti Québécois could hold its own on the North American political scene. There was a full schedule of meetings. In a few hours, he would meet about twenty lenders holding millions of dollars, investors that he had to convince. Lévesque grumbled to himself: "If it were only that!" In the evening, receptions and official handshakes would follow. His personal hell.

∽

"Do they all think the same thing?"

They were rebroadcasting the program in which journalists analysed the premier's visit to the Economic Club.

René Lévesque had committed the error he should have avoided. He had given a disappointing speech! It was the wrong way to speak to the Americans. He turned off the television, lit a cigarette. Were they right in reproaching him for having drawn a parallel between the sovereignty of his country and the thirteen American colonies' struggle for independence? "It was an awkward comparison," Claude Morin remarked to him. "I said to change certain paragraphs." Lévesque was not the type to blame his blunders on others. "Everyone knows that I write my speeches alone." He remained convinced that he was right to mention 1776. Even if the historical context was different from Quebec's, he thought, the people aspiring to freedom displayed the same courage. Drawing inspiration from historian Alexis de Tocqueville, Lévesque maintained that Quebecers were hostage to a political system unfavourable to them. Certainly the parallel was awkward, but he had to find an image for his audience that would hit home. He had managed to shake them up.

"There were one thousand six-hundred guests in the Hilton Ballroom; I'll never believe that they're all as fanatical as the Toronto clique."

2

The Real Quiet Revolution

Monday morning at eight o'clock, Lévesque was at his Quebec City office before the others. The project he was most afraid of was the thorny language law that had to be passed as quickly as possible. He feared that the anglophone community and its representatives who moved in the same circles of high finance would band together against his government. A language law! Of all the Péquistes, Lévesque was one of the most reticent to regulate such a touchy issue. Even though he wished Quebec to be as French as Ontario was English, he wanted anglophones to keep their institutions and their rights. Voting on a language law was putting a bandage on a wound rotting away

René Lévesque opens the Heritage Fair in Longueuil in 1977.

inside. "I want Quebec sovereignty so as to put an end to these quarrels senselessly dividing us."

∽

On the night of February 6, Corinne, on the verge of tears, cried out: "René has just killed a man!"

The accident occurred on Cedar Avenue. Suddenly, in front of him, he saw headlights and a stopped car. A young man was gesturing, signalling for him to avoid something. "What is this nutcase doing here?" Lévesque asked, accelerating. So as not to hit him, he swerved awkwardly to the left. The wheels of the car ran over a body. There was a man lying on the ground – a body on the slippery pavement. Lévesque was convinced that he'd killed him.

The victim, Edgar Trottier, was in his sixties and had no fixed address. On top of everything else – a homeless man! Even though they recognized the premier, police officers showed no favouritism and asked the usual questions. Had Lévesque been drinking too much? Had he made an error in judgment? Had he been absent-minded? Had he been wearing his glasses?

After the euphoria of the November victory, he plummeted to the depths of despair. For a moment, Lévesque thought he was finished. "Should I resign?" This affair contained all the elements of a big scandal. Already, rumour mongers were stressing the fact that the premier had not been alone in the car, but "had been accompanied by his personal secretary." Such innuendo was false. While the English-language press deprecated the premier, the francophone media took pity on him. It wasn't his fault. What was a pedestrian doing on the pavement, anyway? And what about the boy blocking the road, had he done something wrong? In surveys, the majority of respondents accepted the police report. Lévesque had not had too much to drink.

"You're lucky this accident happened at the beginning of your mandate; you're still at the honeymoon stage with journalists," a counsellor remarked to him.

Lévesque could have done without this kind of sympathy. He just wished he'd never lived through such a tragedy.

○

That Wednesday morning the atmosphere in the bunker was strained. The cabinet was discussing a project that Doctor Laurin had dreamed up in secret with specialists on the issue. The cover of this thick file irritated René Lévesque: the hand placing an acute accent on the word "Québec" reminded him of someone slapping the fingers of an insubordinate. From the moment the text was presented, the ministers were at loggerheads: representatives from the Montreal ridings accepted Laurin's work without a second thought. The others were dead against it. Lévesque was caught in the middle of the attacks and insults. Going over the proposed language bill with a fine-toothed comb, he was noncommital. Did his reserved attitude stem partly from his childhood in New Carlisle where he learned to speak English fluently? Meeting supporters of French unilingualism, Lévesque felt no urgency to act, which explained his aggravation as he shouted:

"For heaven's sake, stop frightening everyone by exaggerating so much!"

But at the same time, he added that the Parti Québécois had the right to francize the city because Montreal should no longer have "this bastard face it used to when you couldn't even ask for a pair of socks in French from a saleswoman at Eaton's!" The session rose; they would have to find a middle ground.

The day before presenting the proposed Bill 101 to the National Assembly, René Lévesque summoned Camille Laurin to his office. The problem of signage was bothering him: having language police measure the size of letters to the nearest centimetre in store windows was out of the question. "Our law mustn't prevent little pizzerias with three or four employees from surviving!" Doctor Laurin reassured him; Lévesque returned to the attack. He wanted to suppress Section 73, which said that at the request of either parent, "a child whose father or mother received his or her elementary instruction in English, in Quebec" could receive their instruction in English. He preferred reciprocity, giving anglophones from other provinces the opportunity to study in their language, providing that francophone minorities could enjoy the corresponding rights.

"We are still in Canada; you must not make your proposed legislation more difficult to swallow than sovereignty-association."

The premier rose then sat down, agitated, smoking one cigarette after another.

"Listen up – if a problem arises, you, Camille Laurin, are the one who will suffer the consequences," stated René Lévesque, who urged his minister to go himself and sell his Bill 101 to the people, clearly letting them know that he alone was responsible for this notion.

∽

During its first mandate, aside from the Charter of the French Language and legislation on the financing of political parties, the Péquiste government undertook significant reforms. Suffice it to mention the anti-scab legislation, legislation on occupational health and safety, consumer protection, and agricultural zoning, the creation of the Régie de l'assurance automobile du Québec, and aid to small and medium-sized businesses through the employee stock savings plan. As premier, René Lévesque presided over this energetic social and economic catch-up, but sometimes confessed to his ministers that he would rather trade places with them than be head of state. Fortunately, he was lucky enough to lead diplomatic missions outside Quebec, a role that reminded him of his profession as correspondent. After New York came Paris. The tour of the great capitals continued. But this time, improvising was out of the question. Above all, the premier must not make a gaffe: France had a long aristocratic tradition.

"You will go to Colombey-les-Deux-Églises, of course."

Lévesque remained indifferent. Was it necessary to make this pilgrimage to the tomb of General Charles de Gaulle?

"We'll see – if I have time!"

This reply disconcerted his entourage, but they remained calm. They felt this was "no mere whim," to use the expression employed by Lévesque for ending a pointless discussion. Colombey was a symbolic place; it would be a mistake to head straight to the capital and bypass Lorraine. Hadn't General de Gaulle been the first foreign politician to bring the sovereigntist option to the front pages of international news?

The date was July 24, 1967. The president of the French Republic, during Expo in Montreal, had gone to City Hall. Then, to the amazement of the authorities, he had walked to the balcony where he made an impromptu speech. Carried along by the enthusiasm of the crowd, above a sea of fleurs-de-lis, his final words, distinct and direct, were "Vive le Québec libre!" These four words provoked one of the most commented-upon diplomatic incidents in history. "I was extremely upset," remembered Lévesque who, near the balcony and crouching in front of a television set, had watched the speech broadcast live. Seeking to analyse the impact of this event, he'd been rivetted to the TV screen.

"I said: 'Geez, De Gaulle, is going overboard!' Comparing the euphoria of the Montreal crowd to the Liberation of Paris in 1944 was rather extreme. He was moving fast: in the summer of 1967, the Sovereignty-Association Movement hadn't even been born yet! What I didn't like was that the General, with all due respect, presented himself as a liberator with the idea of decolonizing us. We alone are the ones who will achieve independence, when we want, when the time is right."

Then, after a few seconds went by, he added, grudgingly: "Okay, it's fine. We'll make a stop and visit

Colombey. I'll go meditate at the general's tomb. After all, I do owe him this modest homage."

⌖

Not in ten years had relations between Ottawa and Paris been so strained.

The Canadian Ambassador to France criticized President Valéry Giscard d'Estaing's government for sympathizing with the sovereigntists. He feared above all that René Lévesque would take advantage of this to create special ties with the Élysée palace.

After a few days' vacation in Provence, the Quebec delegation went to Lorraine, where it awaited dignitaries for the ceremony honouring Charles de Gaulle. Television, which followed his every move, scanned the PQ leader from head to toe. The moment the limousine door opened, the camera focused on the guest of honour's feet: René Lévesque was wearing Wallabees!

"Your Monsieur Lévesque is so nice," people said just about everywhere.

His nonchalance had a certain something that captivated those who approached him. He was relaxed – or "cool," to use the in word of the mid-seventies: he came by it naturally. This first trip to France led to the signing of many economic agreements and sealed the friendship between France and Quebec, which had been growing since the late sixties. On this visit, René Lévesque was named Grand Officer of the Légion d'honneur. The ceremony was impressive: beneath the chandeliers of the gilded salon, Valéry Giscard d'Estaing, President of the

Republic, placed the rosette on the lapel of René Lévesque's jacket. Lévesque, uncomfortable with all the pomp and circumstance, thanked him.

"He always wears the same suit," quipped one reporter. "Is it the only one he owns?"

Forced to remain in the background during this trip, not enjoying the privileges of a premier's wife, Corinne was determined that her partner finally decide to divorce so he could marry her.

But Lévesque didn't listen to his companion's complaints; he had other priorities. Time was passing and the deadline for the referendum approaching. In his office, he took stock of his government:

"The real Quiet Revolution is what we're making happen now. And we're the ones who are truly modernizing Quebec. In just one session, we've passed more than twenty-four laws, and not inconsequential ones. I am proud to have helped put an end to the Maurice Duplessis-style messing around in hidden funds. Our law on political party financing is unique, ahead of the times," Lévesque pointed out, a cigarette between his fingers and martini in hand.

Lévesque emphasized the determination of the Department of Consumer Affairs, Cooperatives, and Financial Institutions, which had managed to pass a law on car insurance. No-fault insurance, which guaranteed insurance to all drivers, regardless of whose fault the accident was, was far from receiving unanimous consent in Cabinet. "We made life hard for her," admitted the premier, referring to the minister responsible, Madame Payette. Her courage reminded him of the struggle he himself had led in the sixties to nationalize electricity.

But Lise Payette and René Lévesque had never really hit it off. "He's a male chauvinist," she said. "He looks at women, undressing them from head to toe – and he's no feminist!" And Lévesque replied: "She holds it against me because I say she's moody, but it appears that I am as well."

Like in a classroom where the teacher has favourites, Marc-André Bédard, Minister of Justice, was one of those Lévesque liked most. But the PQ leader's circle of close friends wasn't very large. In any case, those not benefitting from his consideration were better off going unnoticed. The man was caustic, pitiless to any minister not in control of his files. In the caucus, the offender would bear the brunt of Lévesque's wrath. "Go back and do your homework!" he would lash out in front of his colleagues. Time was precious. He knew he could ask a lot of his troops, he who spared no effort in his own work schedule.

∞

"What about the referendum?"

Halfway through his mandate, the question returned with renewed vigour. For two years now, the PQ had shown themselves capable of governing Quebec: the economy was on track and the media were their allies. The social climate was less agitated than under the Liberal government. For example, in 1972, the leaders of three central labour bodies had defied the back to work legislation passed by the Bourassa government. Sentenced to jail, they became heroes and martyrs of the workers' cause. The PQ, learning from the Liberals' mistakes, tried to attract unionized workers and recruited a great many in the public and quasipublic sectors. But this fragile harmony was by no means guaranteed. The PQ had to hold its sovereignty referendum without further ado: procrastination would serve no purpose. The honeymoon between the unions and the Péquistes would end one day; the grace period was fading fast and at a second's notice would be over for good.

∞

In the flying saucer that was the bunker, the cabinet meetings continued to be contentious. As was his habit, Claude Morin would say: "Okay, whose life shall we make difficult today?" In fact, he said aloud what certain people thought to themselves: the government was taking on too much: "we're getting up the backs of many voters who believe we are playing at being socialists."

The gap between the radicals and the conservatives was widening. Fortunately for the PQ, René Lévesque's charisma was still effective. Even when he resolved in favour of one side or another, he managed to make it unanimous. But all the pointless bickering left him perplexed.

"Lévesque embodies our contradictions," remarked Doctor Camille Laurin. "He always seems to be sitting on the fence, unresolved, lukewarm."

∞

That morning, the aroma of burnt toast in the bunker confirmed the PQ leader's presence. With his blackened toast, cup of strong coffee, and omnipresent cigarette, the premier was already at work. He would always remain a journalist. He opened *Le Monde*: in Cambodia, Vietnamese troops had overturned Pol Pot. Keen on international politics, he was interested in what was happening beyond the border. The front page of the *New York Times* described trouble brewing in Iran: the shah was fleeing his country, where Ayatollah Khomeini was being greeted as a redeemer. Quebec's problems didn't hold much weight alongside the human misery festering in the world.

His work finished, he set aside the quarrels of the various factions and quickly began a game of poker! This leaning of his was a source of contention. Certain people insinuated cynically that for Lévesque there were two kinds of members of the Assembly: card players – and others.

"There is a full committee at eight o'clock," Lévesque announced to Marc-André Bédard who understood that that evening they would be playing cards till late in the night.

At the end of the session, René Lévesque gave a press conference. Reporters took notes. Yes, he would go on vacation. Where? He didn't know yet. Before they asked "with whom?" Lévesque rose. There were persistent rumours. Recently divorced, he would not be free for long. On April 12, 1979, the premier tied the knot with Corinne Côté. He was fifty-six, she thirty-five. There would be no more unpleasant incidents like on that winter evening when Madame Barre refused to speak to Monsieur Lévesque's secretary. He married a second time, in order to legalize a union over ten years old. And to please the woman he said he loved fiercely. Fidelity was another story.

After a week in the south of France, it looked as if the return to Quebec would be difficult.

While the Parti Québécois managed to rev up its troops for the referendum deadline, chaos reigned in Ottawa. At the end of March, Pierre Trudeau called an election that he lost on May 22 to the Conservatives. In his office, at the cocktail hour, with his close advisors, René Lévesque gloated:

"Things will be easier with Joe Clark in power."

Trudeau was a thorn in the side of the sovereigntists. The worst was that he had star charisma: he was the man the majority of Quebecers loved, and that others loved to hate. And now he was gone from headlines, no longer undermining the enthusiasm of the Péquistes.

"Certain ministers want us to hold the referendum immediately. They're in a rush. But I'd rather wait a little longer, until the fall or next year."

Lévesque lit another cigarette. A deck of cards on the table. At eight o'clock they played poker.

"Do you wager we'll win this referendum?"

The question was in vain. With Trudeau out of power, the chances of victory had never been so good.

∽

René Lévesque was not prone to effusiveness. He had only cried twice: when Pierre Laporte died, and then more recently, when his mother died.

Diane Dionne had worn the pants in the family. At retirement age, she still travelled. By ship, because she hated airplanes. Alert, independent, after taking language courses, she decided to leave: once for Italy, another time for the Soviet Union.

Lévesque called her "Madame Pelletier" partly to aggravate her, but also because he had never really forgiven his mother for her remarriage to Albert Pelletier, a nationalist lawyer, long since passed away.

The death of his mother and his whole childhood resurfaced, carefree, happy images.

In New Carlisle, on the Baie des Chaleurs, a little boy, wild and free, looking at the ocean, as blue as his eyes.

3

The Son of Maître Lévesque, Esquire

"We'll call him René, like in "renaissance.""
In the hearts of Diane Dionne-Pineault and Dominique Lévesque, their son, born August 24, 1922, in some way replaced André, the elder brother, who had died prematurely.

Custom would have dictated that they name him for his godfather, John Hall Kelly, an Irishman, powerful financier, and Bonaventure County politician, who was his father's partner in the law firm they had opened together.

Nowadays, when René Lévesque wanted to amuse his family, he proclaimed himself John Lévesque, sovereigntist premier! Tit-Jean, to close friends. "I had a narrow escape!" he would add.

René Lévesque, age three.

René Lévesque, student of rhetoric
at Collège Garnier in Quebec City.

Remembering his childhood, René Lévesque compared francophones' social inequality to that then suffered by the blacks in Rhodesia: "we were colonized: the good schools, the nice homes, all the wealth was in the hands of people who identified with the victors of the Conquest."

But in New Carlisle, the Lévesques were not exactly poor French Canadians. True, the first house they lived in, on rue Principale, facing the sea, had no running water, but this lack of resources didn't last long. Dominique Lévesque was a gifted lawyer. He had charm and managed to make a name for himself. In 1925, he announced to his wife that he had the twenty-three hundred dollars needed to buy a fine house at auction, at the corner of Mount Sorel and Second Streets. The white wooden house had a large balcony and a sloping roof. The windows of the upstairs rooms looked out over the Baie des Chaleurs. A view to make a small, unruly boy dream. Constantly fidgeting, he was such a handful that sometimes his mother had to fasten him to a post of the staircase.

"It's time we send René to Rivière-du-Loup," decreed Diane, who needed rest, having given birth to three more children after René, the eldest.

Staying with his grandparents was no punishment. He loved taking the train, with its rustic cars, a railway reminiscent of movie westerns. How grand to be free, play at selling penny candy in Grandpa's general store, and to see Grandma again.

"René," she would say affectionately: "let's have a game of poker. If you lose your dollar, we'll cancel the debt. But if you win…"

Clever and astute, René often won the kitty and left for New Carlisle with his card winnings like a jackpot in his pocket. His taste for gambling he derived from his grandmother Alice. The sound of cards being shuffled, the waiting, heart pounding – little by little he began to love this exquisite moment when anything was possible. There was a thin line between winning and losing: he was walking a tightrope. He calculated his chances, then took a wholehearted leap into the unknown.

René Lévesque would remain a gambler his entire life.

⌒

"The most important man in my life." In 1986, René Lévesque dedicated his memoirs to his father Dominique. In New Carlisle, the well-known lawyer was his son's hero. The two resembled one another. A love of books brought them together. In this city at the world's end, the train brought in the newspapers when the snow wasn't falling too heavily. They would throw themselves on the *Montreal Standard* and attack the crossword puzzles, ready to compete. Who would be first to finish filling in the boxes? To lose was humiliating.

"It's not fair; you speak better English than I do," the son would sulk; "after all, your clients write to you in English."

He had observed that the father's correspondence was addressed to Dominique Lévesque, Esq. Where did this unusual title come from? "Esquire" – a word found in the work of Jacques Ferron – used to mean a squire of the minor nobility. Here, the title simply meant "Mister." As dictated by the sociolinguistic context, "Esquire" seemed chic because it sounded like English. In such an environment it was quite natural that from a very young age René was bilingual: when little English kids shouted at him "pea soup! pea soup!" he answered them back in their language, throwing pebbles at them.

Defiant and impudent, he would run from the forest to the sea. Paspébiac Point was his kingdom. He was fearless. In September he went to the country school and thought about what he would do on Saturday afternoon. In the church hall, the parish priest had just announced they would show a movie.

"*Jungle Princess* with Dorothy Lamour!"

He was on cloud nine. For days, he would go around softly singing the refrain: "I love you, you love me." His little heart throbbed for the beautiful Hollywood star and even harder for the mermaid of Baie des Chaleurs who, the week before, had saved him from drowning.

His true childhood ended abruptly in September 1933: his luggage ready, the next day, he would leave for the Séminaire de Gaspé. René was to follow in his father's footsteps and become a lawyer, according to his mother's wishes. One thing was certain: he would not be a priest, for he had no religious leanings. For him the seminary was above all a place of intellectual discovery, which made him eager to hop aboard the train, to go away, to try his wings.

The journey was long and rather uncomfortable: for five hours, he watched the scenery go by. Gaspé was so far, it seemed as if the public officials had forgotten it. For the Mi'Kmaq people, Gaspé meant the end, the extremity. The tip of the country. When he got off the train, René had arrived at the end of his journey, at the dawn of a new life.

At the seminary, the young student distinguished himself from the others. While the majority swotted for hours, he devoted only about twenty minutes a day to his work. Afterwards, he would shut himself up in the library, where he combed the shelves for biographies of famous men. History fascinated him. Professors spoke of this teenager as a future leader. He was one of the few who didn't like hockey, far preferring tennis, at which he excelled. At age fourteen, he won the Gaspé Junior Championship. On the court he ran easily to the net, his serve impeccable. An ace!

The Lévesque family supported the reds, in memory of Liberal Sir Wilfrid Laurier, the French Canadian born in Saint-Lin who succeeded in governing Canada for fifteen years. What an achievement! In the mid nineteen-thirties Mackenzie King was the heir apparent worthy of his illustrious predecessor, while his provincial counterpart, Louis-Alexandre Taschereau, was becoming embroiled in scandals exposed by Maurice Duplessis, the member from Trois-Rivières. People even went so far as to predict that on August 17, the Union Nationale, which he had just founded, would sweep the province. In 1936, René was a teenager who had landed a summer job at a radio station. Not a fan of politics, he nevertheless attended a meeting held in the area, and, excitedly reported to his father that he had gone to see Philippe Hamel, the leader of the Action libérale nationale.

"He's a politician with some strange ideas: he wants to nationalize electricity companies. He's taken up Reverend Groulx's slogan, *Maîtres chez nous*, Masters in our own house. Do you think that could ever come to pass?"

∽

Dominique Lévesque was a shadow of the man he'd been. Thin, prematurely aged, and in pain, he had to be driven to Campbellton Hospital. His condition was more serious than originally thought: he would receive better care in Quebec City. Suitcases were packed. In June 1937, just returned home, René saw his father leave.

"You are the eldest. Take care of your mother, and your brothers, Fernand and André. Your little sister Alice will also need you. When I come home, we'll go to the seashore and look for twenty-five-cent lobsters, the way we do every summer."

There was no reason that the New Carlisle lawyer should not return; he was only forty-eight years old.

∽

In *The Ocean*, the legendary train following the voyageur route right to the Atlantic, René looked out the window at the calm river in the moonlight. Sleep remained elusive. He had a sense of foreboding. What did it mean? In Rivière-du-Loup, his grandparents met him at the station. There was no longer any need to go to Quebec City. Dominique Lévesque was dead.

It was his first great sorrow. An absence never to be filled. The father's presence was forever etched in his memory and gestures, such as the son's odd habit of holding a pencil between his index and middle fingers. Dominique had also written like that.

∞

The year was 1937. His last at the seminary. Showered with prizes and distinctions, René, who still didn't know what he would do later, was dismayed to learn he would not be returning to New Carlisle. His mother had moved to Quebec City and was going to marry Albert Pelletier, a family friend. For the young man, this was an insult! Given the opportunity, René would have thrown himself immediately into journalism. Obliged to finish his classical education, he enrolled at Collège Saint-Charles-Garnier, an institution for sons from good families. It was a shock. For the first time, he felt as if in exile. He wrote in the student newspaper: "I am the boy from the Gaspé, feeling like a fish out of water." His schoolmates got on his nerves; he found their narrow-mindedness irritating. "Everything has been handed to them on a silver platter. They don't know how to be charitable." The people he made friends with were artists. As he liked to write, he penned articles for the student newspaper. People read him, talked about him. He enjoyed success. But he still remained on the fringes of what to him was a foreign world. He didn't complain. His mind was elsewhere.

∽

At the Marceau's, where a lively crowd gathered, René would spend hours playing cards with the mistress of the house, an Irishwoman impassioned about the subject of her country of origin's political situation.

"You're like a second mother to me," he confided to her one day.

"And you René, are my fifteenth child!"

These were repressive times. While Cardinal Villeneuve had forbidden dancing, calling it "a sin," in the Marceau family, girls were allowed to meet boys. A seventy-eight on the record player, Frank Sinatra, "The Voice," sang Cole Porter: "I've got you under my skin." That evening, a relaxed young man, cigarette dangling from his lips, noticed a pretty brunette dancing the swing. She was Louise L'Heureux, daughter of the publisher of *L'Action catholique*, a Quebec City daily.

"I've seen you before, at the St. Dominique skating rink. My name is René Lévesque, may I have the next dance?"

When he wrapped his arm around her waist, the two made an entrancing couple. It was the beginning of a romance unthreatened by any cloud.

∽

On September 3, 1939, Great Britain and France declared war on Germany, whose army had invaded Poland two days earlier. Until May 1940, it had been a waiting game, the phoney war, as it was called. Then came news from the front: disaster. The French army's losses were mounting.

At seventeen, René Lévesque turned away from his studies, adopting the credo "life is what you make it!" When forbidden to smoke, he slammed the door and went to join his friends at cards. His mother kicked up a fuss: Dominique Lévesque's eldest son would never be a lawyer like his father. With average grades, he avoided coming last, thanks to his quick memory. Nervous, undisciplined, he thought himself infallible until the day the rector of the Collège handed him a letter expelling him. He enrolled in Laval University in September 1941, but it was merely an interlude, a way to delay leaving his studies for good.

I'm a vingt cennes from Valcartier... On the radio, Soldier Roland Lebrun sang about the daily existence of poor recruits peeling potatoes in Valcartier. Meanwhile, young Lévesque was leading the life of a bohemian, hair tousled, sloppily dressed. He hung out on the Plains of Abraham, flirted with girls, smoked his last cigarette down to the butt. Life went by, calm, meaningless, while in Old Quebec the young soldiers got ready to board a ship for Europe.

4

Seeing the War First Hand

"I leave tomorrow."

May 1944. In uniform, boots freshly polished, a kepi jammed tightly on his head, René Lévesque made his entrance in the living room on rue de Laune. Who would have thought that the lazybones of Collège Garnier would one day be a soldier? His mother was distraught at the thought her son could die on a beach in Normandy, just like the unnamed who gave their lives in Dieppe in August 1942.

"I've signed up in the American army. I won't have to kill Germans. No! I am a war correspondent."

What a great idea! As opposed to volunteers and draftees, he would not have to take orders from an

In 1944-1945, René Lévesque, who enlisted in the American army, worked as a war correspondent in England.

English-Canadian commander. Any day now, the Canadian army's Board of Review was liable to call in René Lévesque for a physical. Without a sympathetic doctor, he would be unable to escape mobilization. How could he get out of this mess? Lévesque could not picture himself as a tommy under the Union Jack. A lowly French Canadian serviceman – never! Then he came up with the brilliant idea of getting in touch with Phil Robb at the American Office of War Information. *In Uncle Sam's army*, he thought, *I won't be on the front lines.* And as he was bilingual, he could hope to become an interpreter by translating news releases for the Americans.

When Lévesque obtained his visa, the world conflict had taken a new twist: the U.S. had finally entered the war that Roosevelt had every intention of winning.

René Lévesque was twenty-one years old and ready to see the war up close, without actually fighting. There were still risks, of course. Overseas, the Germans continued to drop their bombs. Certainly he was scared, but not enough to back out. In a last letter to his mother, he boasted: "I'm leaving on a cruise with over five thousand dollars in my pocket!"

He was grandstanding, for he knew that this trip would be nothing like an ocean holiday.

∞

On Pier Number 4, about twenty passengers were boarding the *Indochinois*. As he smoked, René Lévesque leaned on the ship's rail and gazed at the sky. Under a starless sky, enshrouded in fog, the city slept.

A Hitchcockian atmosphere, like in *The Secret Agent*, which he had recently seen in a small movie theatre on Ste-Catherine Street. Another cigarette. The previous year German U-boats had blown up about thirty Allied ships. He turned up the collar of his jacket. The signal to depart sounded. He told himself that as they were passing Quebec he would think of his mother, his brothers and sister, and of Louise, his fiancée, whom he'd promised to marry upon his return. All being equal. Meanwhile, she would have to be patient. "I'll write, darling. I promise!" The playboy would think of Louise, all the while seducing other girls, such as Bernice, who went back to her native Yorkshire. She was so cute!

∽

At the American Broadcasting Station in Europe, René Lévesque read encoded messages that resembled the finely wrought corpses of the surrealists. Although he liked his work, he enjoyed playing cards at Bistro Chez Auguste even more. His passion for card playing followed him everywhere. At that time, the London sky was a battleground. At any moment they feared the Blitz, the air war of attrition, which the English were subjected to from September 7 to November 2, 1940.

In the night, there were more bombs. The situation no longer felt like a movie where the hero triumphs over the bad guys. Today his own building superintendent was in tears, praying that the enemy bombers would spare them.

∽

On the airwaves of the BBC, Vera Lynn sang *The White Cliffs of Dover*. London, with its big black taxis, its red double-decker buses, and Big Ben sounding the passing of time, had never been so nostalgic. Crossing Hyde Park, Lévesque observed a gathering. Was it a military demonstration? A Hindu with a long beard, his thin body imprisoned in a white shroud, was forecasting all sorts of evil for the British Empire. Such a scene would be unimaginable in Quebec. "We are the victims of our own bickering," wrote Lévesque to his family. In fact, this stay in England would emancipate him, open horizons. When his mother announced she intended to vote for Maurice Duplessis, he replied: "No, don't!" He even advised her to abstain, though as a woman, this was the first time she could exercise her right to vote. To Lévesque, the man they derisively referred to as "le cheuf" – "the chief" – embodied an old political guard whose time was long since past.

∽

René Lévesque had certainly not crossed the Atlantic to get stuck in some mindless, bureaucratic job. Playing cards and winning British pounds by bluffing was boring. And there was nothing seductive about the girls here, with their overly long skirts. Don Juan was discouraged. One day, he received the news he was hoping for: his visa for France had come through.

Age twenty-two, Junior Lieutenant René Lévesque joined up with General Omar Bradley's 12th Army Group. Later he would join up with General Patton. A real adventure!

On the continent, the war was far from over. Junior Lieutenant Lévesque, pen in hand, was a witness to the death rattle of the Nazi madness. The suicidal fanatics who had taken up arms did not surrender. German soldiers, abandoned by SS headquarters, had nothing left to lose. Forty kilometres from Strasbourg, Lévesque took refuge in a vineyard. It was cold and rainy. Conditions were repulsive. There was no hygiene, no way to warm themselves when the wind arose. Beneath their khaki coats, the men shivered, collars turned up to their ears. "That's where I lost my voice," René Lévesque later confided. Untreated laryngitis, flu, headaches: his body had never suffered so. Did he fear for his life? In his letters, he chose to emphasize his companions' bravery. Between the Free French Forces and the Americans, Lévesque was the Canuck. Resourceful, taking full advantage of his privileged status that shielded him from personal conflict, he acted as a go-between for the two camps. When he returned to General Patton's division, he nevertheless had the impression that soon he would no longer manage to escape the horror. In May 1945, his unit entered a German city unfamiliar to him: Dachau.

∽

"Konzentrationlager?"

A Bavarian farmer leaned over the Americans' olive-coloured jeep and pointed to a road straight ahead. Dachau wasn't far off, near those houses, strangely still intact, which conjured up images of families sitting down to dinner. At first glance, a city like any other. But the closer they got, the more agonizing the sight of the devastation. Here, Allied bombs had blown up buildings, and smoke still escaped from the rubble and stone. There, a wasteland, where it looked as if buildings had been levelled. On the road, strangers pulled carts filled with all they had left. Women and children were crying, begging. But the jeep continued on its path. At the end, hell. The concentration camps.

Railway tracks crossed each other leading up to the camp entrance. Control towers loomed on all four sides. The American jeep passed wrought iron gates that gave onto a large open space. On either side, buildings with blank walls were partially obscured by convoys of abandoned trains. Along with his companions, Junior Lieutenant Lévesque got out of the vehicle. Skeletal bodies in striped pyjamas came out of the buildings to throw themselves on the liberators. The troops had deserted, leaving behind human beings in living conditions worse than for cattle. Dachau, Buchenwald – the horror was everywhere. Lévesque jotted down the answers of a French prisoner to whom he'd given a cigarette. How to describe the unspeakable? The roundups of the *Geheime Staatspolizei*, the Gestapo, the selections of the deportees. And the Jews, wearing the yellow star, a number tattooed on their forearms, forced into cattle cars that wound up here.

Being a war correspondent meant exposing injustice, explaining it, whistle-blowing. It was listening to a survivor who indicated, in the distance, the superimposed wooden cages that served as beds. Over there, prisoners had perished in the gas chambers disguised to resemble showers. "In back, on the mound, was the firing squad." Farther on, another building: "the crematory ovens where they brought women and children."

Suddenly they heard shouting coming from close by. The prisoners had discovered a German soldier who had hidden in a bush: "A kapo! A kapo!" The former executioner was on his knees, begging for mercy. With the pitiless strength of vengeance, a stunned-looking man whacked him on the jaw. He attacked the body, savage, unrelenting. Soon the man was but a mass of bloody flash. "What could we have done?" Lévesque asked himself.

For a long time he would carry this war silently within himself, for he feared that words would betray his disgust in mankind. Haunted by what he had seen in Dachau, fired up by democratic ideals, Lévesque had no illusions about the meaning of the word *humanity*. At this juncture his revulsion for extremism began to take hold, leading him to seek moderation in everything. After witnessing the death camps, René Lévesque believed that a journalist's mission was to awaken people's consciences. Journalism was the vocation he wanted to pursue.

5

A Passion for Communicating

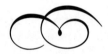

In the port of Quebec City, as René Lévesque disembarked, his family was there to greet him. What was the news in Europe? Wasn't he one of the rare people to have gone right into Adolf Hitler's eagle's nest shortly before the defeat of Germany? From his luggage, he took out a record *Lili Marlene*; the sleeve featured a faded autograph, virtually illegible. He had found this treasure in the rubbish.

"In Milan, I saw Mussolini and his mistress Clara Petacci, whose corpses had been hung upside down. The crowd, who before had worshipped them, rushed forward to shout abuse at the corpses."

Travelling broadens horizons. Although everything seemed the same, new inspiration was sweeping

Archives nationales du Québec à Montréal/P48, S1, P23495.

René Lévesque, a journalist at Radio-Canada, reading a text
at the microphone at the Cercle des journalistes de Montréal,
in June 1949.

National Archives of Canada/C-077793.

In 1951, René Lévesque travelled to South Korea
as a reporter for Radio-Canada.

through Quebec. Meanwhile, Maurice Duplessis, in power since 1944, reigned unopposed. The province had never been so blue, which was the colour of the Union Nationale, its supporters, and its clique.

As for Lévesque, he was interested in the geopolitics transforming the planet. In August 1945, American President Harry Truman dropped the atomic bomb on Hiroshima and Nagasaki. Then, at the Yalta Conference, Stalin divided borders as if slicing a cake: this piece of Poland for him, the crumbs for the others. International news fascinated René Lévesque. "It seems as if what's happening here leaves you cold," a friend reproached him.

Communicating was his passion, and radio was the most effective medium. But there was a catch. An announcer needed to have a pleasant voice. Lévesque could never compete with Roger Baulu, François Bertrand, or René Lecavalier. So what! His years of experience would compensate for his shortcomings. He had guts and charm. Would he abandon his legal studies? René remained deaf to his mother's arguments, she who dreamed of seeing him follow in his father's footsteps.

"Radio-Canada pays me twenty-seven hundred dollars a year – I've struck it rich! I'm moving to Montreal."

This put an end to Diane's complaints. She conceded defeat.

∽

In the studio, Lévesque awaited the signal from his producer. Taking the microphone, he announced in an assured voice:

"This is the voice of Canada, Montreal, Canada."

It was 7:00 p.m. in France. Hired as an announcer, Lévesque introduced the program *Les Actualités canadiennes*, a news show about Canada. At twenty-four, he knew the ins and outs of the profession: reading the papers, doing special features and interviews. Lévesque joined an enthusiastic team, a group of artists who spent weekends on the tennis courts. So much for his fiancée Louise, whom he had promised to marry before he left for Europe. He never had any trouble finding a companion to go with him to the movies or the theatre, for example, the attractive, rather cool and distant intellectual who worked at Radio-Canada. Employed by the international service, she was downright seductive.

"I'm also an actress, by the way. Since 1938, I've been playing Élise Velder in Robert Choquette's *La pension Velder*."

Judith Jasmin was six years René Lévesque's senior. Both had a passion for journalism and were well-educated, inquisitive, and somewhat ironical. They were made for one another.

Louise was growing impatient: for over a year now, her fiancé, René, seemed to be happy playing the single man. He in Montreal, she in Quebec City: time was passing, and with it, the likelihood of marriage. If he could, Lévesque would avoid tying the knot. A born seducer, flirting came naturally to him. It was a game. His mind was not on love, and he declared: "What I saw in Europe has remained with me. Dachau, the prisoners on the roads, the mindless masses, their uncontrollable hatred." His work at the radio station devoured his time and energy; marital responsibilities would get in the way of his plans.

For a while, he managed to stave off the day he would marry. But his promises caught up with him: on May 3, 1947, he married Louise L'Heureux in Quebec City in a small ceremony. The young marrieds were in a hurry to leave for Virginia Beach, where they would lie on the sand and swim in the ocean.

When they returned, they settled in Montreal, and the birth of a son strengthened family ties. But gradually Lévesque deserted family life, for he far preferred the excitement of being a journalist.

Because his employers didn't have enough faith in him, he made it known that he wanted to leave the international service. He hated being limited to routine tasks. A workaholic, he would shut himself up in the library for days at a time, taking notes on what was happening in the world, drawing his information from the American and French press at a time when few colleagues were that eclectic. Lévesque was convinced that his talent would be recognized. That day was not far off.

∞

When in January 1948 Quebec obtained its own flag, the Fleur-de-lis, Lévesque was more concerned with Harry Truman's re-election: he was angry at the Americans for putting this hillbilly in his Sunday best back in power.

Canadian politics were so dull! Louis Saint-Laurent, called "Uncle Louis," successor to Mackenzie King, perpetuated the Liberal tradition in Ottawa. Quebec politics were a bore! Although he harshly criticized Maurice Duplessis, who ruled the province with an iron hand, René Lévesque maintained a distance from the upcoming social reforms. In August 1948, young artists connected with painter Paul-Émile Borduas published *Refus global*. They denounced the religion that was suffocating French Canadian society and blamed political authorities for their lies and betrayals. Forced to resign from his job at the École du meuble, Borduas went into exile in Paris, where he died in 1961. Judith Jasmin, who knew actress Muriel Guilbault and poet Claude Gauvreau well, often spoke of her polemical friends.

But Lévesque was wary of these fiery idealists and unaffected by their anger.

Now a news announcer at the international service, he wanted to be elsewhere. The Korean War would give him that opportunity.

On June 25, 1950, five North Korean divisions crossed the 38th parallel to attack the South Korean capital, Seoul. It would take only one spark to re-ignite the fire that had been smouldering since the end of the Second World War. The UN Security Council condemned North Korea's aggression at the very moment that President Truman ordered sending over American troops. Under General Douglas MacArthur's command, the UN combatants drove back Kim II Sung's North Korean troops to the Chinese border.

These events so impassioned Lévesque that unionist Jean Marchand, one of his most skilled poker partners, couldn't help but reproach him for knowing more about the Asian peninsula than his own country.

"Last year," he said, bluffing at cards, "you didn't even support the asbestos strikers beaten up by Duplessis's police."

"I work at Radio-Canada, I have to remain neutral," replied Lévesque, who described himself as "semi-rootless."

∞

Lévesque scored a significant coup: fascinated by the Korean War, he succeeded one day in interviewing a soldier who had been part of the Canadian Battalion under UN command. On his hospital bed, the wounded man confided that young Americans on the line of fire wanted only to return home as soon as possible. René Lévesque found the right tone: his feature dealt with what was happening at the time. When Radio-Canada offered him a position as war correspondent in Korea, he was sorry he wasn't free, "otherwise, I'd leave this instant!"

The father of two endured his wife's wrath: "What? You would leave home for six months?" Louise said to him, incredulous. But would René turn down his employers' offer? No one could make him change his mind. In July 1951, he announced to those close to him:

"I have my visa in hand and am leaving in a few days."

∽

The armed forces vehicle headed deeper into the jungle. Direction: no man's land, in the vicinity of the Imjin River, an isolated area straight out of a John Wayne movie. But this was real life. Holed up in a tent, between a pallet and a lopsided table, René Lévesque set up camp; this served as his studio. Now he was ready to make history come alive. Thousands of kilometres from Quebec, he would tell the listeners of Radio-Canada what he had experienced.

His direct, sincere style shocked people. His rasping voice and nervous phrasing became his trademark. People listened to René Lévesque. Radio was a media form still in its youth, and Lévesque did away with the old-fashioned, heavy-handed style that so far had prevailed. He followed a Canadian battalion on the trail of Chinese ambushes. Chilled to the bone as the rain fell, he shared the soldiers' fear; he too stalked the enemy that was advancing, bayonets in hand. He slung a tape recorder over his shoulder and gathered testimonies of actors in a play without any *deus ex machina* to come to the rescue. Lévesque invented radio vérité. On his program *A Sunday in Korea with the 22nd Regiment*, he spoke with a soldier who missed Lac du Sapin Croche, where he liked to go fishing.

The Korean War dragged on. Death was everywhere. As for Lévesque, he received letters from his wife imploring him to return home. Wasn't it unfair to leave his family all alone? In September 1951, he returned to Montreal. That early autumn felt like spring in Dorval.

∞

René Lévesque was determined to leave the international service; now he wanted to switch to national radio. People could tell him time and again that he wasn't as elegant as the in-house announcers, that he possessed neither their diction nor their vocal quality, but his ambition never wavered.

After Asia, he was entrusted with covering the royal visit of Princess Elizabeth and Prince Philip. The British monarchy was then at its peak and Radio-Canada was the place to be during the royal tour of Canada. For Lévesque, this assignment was pure pleasure. His head was in the clouds. Accompanied by Judith Jasmin – who had become infatuated with him and hoped he would leave his wife so they could live out their storybook romance – he covered these special events as if he were on honeymoon. The management of Radio-Canada, shocked by his free-and-easy attitude, called him to order.

∞

The remonstrations left Lévesque indifferent. From then on, he had but one idea: becoming a part of the team that would launch television in Canada, on September 6, 1952.

At first glance, Lévesque seemed perfect for the opening ceremonies. But disappointment was in store:

the honour went to Judith Jasmin. He had to wait a little longer before finally hosting a public affairs program: *Carrefour*. Modelled on the type of interview given by Joseph Morrow – the most popular American host at the time – his interviews portrayed politicians in a new light.

On the dawn of the Quiet Revolution, television was a gateway to stardom. René Lévesque made his mark there, for he knew how to take advantage of the medium. But he constantly had to do battle with Radio-Canada management, who persisted in not giving him a prominent role. Exasperated by their refusals, he agreed to forego his rights as a regular employee in order to host a program closer to his heart.

On Sunday, October 28, 1956, the credits rolled at eleven fifteen: *Point de mire* was on the air.

The idea was René Lévesque's. So was the title, meaning "focus." The set was simple: a table, a blackboard, and a map of the world. Each week, holding a piece of chalk like a teacher in front of a classroom, Lévesque analysed a key event or problem in the news. One evening, he talked about the Suez Canal, which Nasser wanted to nationalize. The next week, pointer in hand, he delineated the borders of Hungary, which the Soviet Union's tanks had just invaded.

A legend was born. Of course, the audience ratings of *Point de mire* never reached those of *Hockey Night in Canada* nor of *La famille Plouffe*, but this program had the rare quality of opening up Quebec to other horizons. International news, television's poor relation, became for the first time a controversial subject. In 1958, René Lévesque was propelled to the forefront of the news when he left to cover the referendum in Algeria. His feature stories were lessons in history. In the streets of Algiers, as if in Montreal, he let unknowns speak. With him, the image of the global village became clearer, and viewers understood that the problems of the planet affected them at home. The success of *Point de mire* was not happenstance; a great deal of work went into it, beginning in the library, where Lévesque shut himself up for hours to sift through newspapers and encyclopedias. His proven method was to take notes, then edit and rewrite them until he was satisfied.

"Ready, René?"

Producer Claude Sylvestre was approaching with the plan: Sunday morning there would be a final meeting before taping – providing no major event popped up in the news!

A freelancer at Radio-Canada, René Lévesque earned sixteen thousand dollars a year, double what his colleagues were pulling in. He liked his team and moreover had free rein over the topics for *Point de mire*. He was on a roll. The father of three blew in and out of the house like a whirlwind. His work monopolized him and his love affairs were mere flings. He told himself that he could remain in this profession a long time: he hadn't reckoned on events that would turn his certainties upside down.

René Lévesque, Minister of Natural Resources in Jean Lesage's
Liberal government, opens an exhibit of Inuit art
at the Queen Elizabeth Hotel in 1964.

6

Minister in the Lesage Government

A t five o'clock in the afternoon of December 29, 1958, in the lobby of the Ford Building, a union leader ordered "Everyone out!" Seventy-four Radio-Canada producers immediately gathered on the sidewalk of Dorchester Boulevard. It was cold. The strikers rubbed their hands together to keep warm. They were demanding the right to unionize, and they criticized their employers, whose head office was in Toronto, for ignoring the demands of the French service and seeing Montreal as an outpost. In 1958, Radio-Canada was the Canadian Broadcasting Corporation, CBC.

The first day of the conflict, René Lévesque was in his office. He was growing impatient: where was his

producer? Time was running short, *Point de mire* had
to start taping in a few minutes. Glancing outside, he
recognized Claude Sylvestre:

"What? He's in the street with the others?...
Those idiots!"

His anger was matched only by his frustration:
naturally enough, he was afraid of losing his benefits.
Just when he had managed to put a program on the air
that was tailor-made for him, chaos erupted. Of course
he was sympathetic to producers' demands, but since
going freelance, he was on the sidelines of battles
being waged between Radio-Canada administrators
and employees. People asked him to take a stand. He
curtly replied that he had no intention of becoming
embroiled in the strike. "It's none of my business!" At
home, his wife convinced him to remain neutral. He
had three young children, and his family obligations
forced him to remain loyal to his employers, who had
just signed him to a very profitable contract.

There was an explanation for Lévesque's apparent
indifference. Entangled in love affairs, he panicked
when he learned that one of his mistresses had just
given birth to a child. Leading a double life was causing
problems. On top of his personal troubles came work
troubles. Little by little, public life took hold of him
and offered a means of escape.

At the beginning of 1959, the Radio-Canada producers' strike was a tunnel with no light at the end. The
strikers had been battling the cold, stamping their feet
in front of the Ford Building for two weeks now.
Would they have to spend the winter outdoors?
Management thought it could wear them down. As

consolation, the producers told themselves that they had the support of the Union des artistes, whose members were asked not to cross picket lines. In mid-January, to make up for salary losses, a fundraiser was organized: they staged a benefit show that surpassed all expectations. At the Comédie canadienne, the public rushed to see Denise Pelletier dance the mambo and to applaud Olivier Guimond in a burlesque number. *Difficultés temporaires* was such a smash that they decided to take it on tour.

"Join us," they asked René Lévesque once more, and he ended up agreeing.

Between two routines, the journalist-star resurrected *Point de mire*. On the blackboard, he explained why Radio-Canada producers wanted their association to be recognized. He accused Toronto of letting down the "natives." Lévesque was successful. His arguments came at the right time; with simple words, he managed to stir up the audience.

But one show could not a conflict settle. After going to Parliament Hill in Ottawa to demonstrate their dissatisfaction, the strikers organized a meeting in Montreal. More than sixty days had passed since management had turned a deaf ear to the producers' demands. René Lévesque was now one of their most ardent supporters. At the Théatre du Gésu, he harangued strikers. Was it he who incited them to storm the doors of the Ford Building?

"He's an agitator!" a police inspector would say of him.

Hadn't he been seen leading a group that walked down Bleury Street to take Dorchester? Alerted, the police blocked the path of the demonstrators. In the crush, people were injured. Some demonstrators struck up *O Canada* while megaphones blasted the message to "keep moving! keep moving!" Wedged in, the strikers couldn't move. Jammed into the paddy wagon with about twenty others, Lévesque knew that he had just mortgaged his future at Radio-Canada; management would probably remove him from *Point de mire*. The next day, a photograph appeared in newspapers: a full-face shot of a man, looking both insolent and stunned, a tuque pulled down over his ears.

René Lévesque was leaving prison. He was entering history.

∞

The death of Premier Maurice Duplessis on September 7, 1959, followed by that of his successor Paul Sauvé one hundred days later, disconcerted the Union Nationale. Antonio Barrette, who then took over, called upon voters to legitimize his mandate. With the provincial election slated for June 22, 1960, a whirlwind campaign began that made it look as if the old world were dying out. Jean Lesage was determined to rise to power, and he sought outstanding men. He wanted to create a Liberal dream team or an "équipe du tonnerre," an expression that would designate the group he was putting together. In his Windsor Hotel headquarters in Montreal, the Liberal leader noted names of those he'd like to have with him: Jean Marchand, a fiery union leader and opponent of Duplessis during the Asbestos strike; Gérard Pelletier, a talented journalist and noted intellectual; and Pierre Elliott Trudeau, professor of constitutional law, a blue-blood, and moreover, bilingual.

Lesage was open about his preferences. Any one of the three – or better still, the three together – would be a good move for the Quebec Liberal Party.

"And you, René, would you be tempted to take the plunge into politics?" Jean Marchand asked him one day. "I spoke of you, sang your praises. The Liberals would like to meet you."

Would Lévesque consider entering an election campaign that he could lose? He drained a last scotch, stubbed out his cigarette. "Goodbye Jean, see you next week!" Lévesque put on his coat. Reflected briefly for a moment. He pushed open the door. When he reached the lobby, he turned around and went back to Jean Lesage's office. He had not prepared any speech, but simply said:

"Monsieur Lesage, here I am! I will agree to what-ever riding you choose to give me. I want to be a part of your team."

Winning the riding of Montreal-Laurier was by no means assured: René Lévesque had to compete in a Union Nationale stronghold, whose legacy included Duplessis-type methods of persuasion. Questionable tactics were used. With his television-star aura, Lévesque shook things up. Early on in the campaign, people attacked both the man and his ideas: "He's a communist... he met Nikita Khrushchev." The memory of his trip to Moscow more than five years earlier dogged him, even reaching meetings of the Union Nationale. The accusation was so far-fetched that it ended up backfiring on those who had perpetrated it.

An election is first and foremost a game of seduction. On this score, Lévesque had no problem. While people criticized his raspy voice, coarse manners, and long, colourful sentences adorned by extraordinary metaphors, when he went from door to door they recognized him, congratulating him on what he was doing at *Point de mire*. The man was likeable. People admired his achievements, audacity, and intelligence. While on the campaign trail, Lévesque was accompanied by wrestler Johnny Rougeau, an imposing hulk of a man. Despite the contrast in appearance between the bodyguard and the candidate for the Quebec legislature, work and friendship brought them together.

"Have you seen the dirty trick they're trying to play?"

The candidate for the legislature learned that, to confuse voters, his opponents had come up with a man whose name was the same as his: in Montreal-Laurier, two René Lévesques would be running. Voters would have to be careful to avoid making a mistake. Would he lose the riding over something so insignificant? "Elections are not won by prayers," Israel Tarte had said. The Union Nationale and the Liberal Party were not afraid to use dubious methods in order to secure seats in the legislature. Businessmen had established their kingdom in Laurier. "If I win," promised René Lévesque, I'll put an end to hidden funds." He had entered politics in order to bring Quebec into the modern era. Duplessis-style bribery was a thing of the past; Lévesque embodied a dynamic and youthful style of politics.

In 1960, winning was not a sure thing for Lévesque, who wondered whether the team's slogan, *It's time for a change*, would strike a chord with Quebecers.

On June 22, people impatiently awaited the election results. At the end of the evening, victory was assured by a majority of eight ridings: Premier Lesage appeared beneath photographers' flashbulbs and the spotlights of national television. At Liberal headquarters on St. Hubert Street, René Lévesque was jubilant. He had won the Laurier riding. But his margin was so slim – barely 129 votes – that it took another two weeks to complete the recount. On July 4 he knew that he would go to Quebec City, but not as a backbencher... he wanted no less than to be a minister.

∞

Even if he liked him a great deal, Jean Lesage did not want René Lévesque too much underfoot. The member from Laurier was indomitable. From the very start, he had confided to his leader: "I don't want to become Minister of Old Age!" A dig at the Department of Social Welfare, which went to someone else. Lesage assigned him to Hydroelectric Resources and Public Works, a job that suited him. In the Red Room, when preparing to sign the formal documents, Lévesque told himself he could finally carry out projects near to his heart.

First, he would get rid of the old mentality, short-sighted favouritism. Minister Lévesque insisted that henceforth contracts for bridge and road construction be put to public tender. He imposed rules of respect-able conduct. Abhorring petty politics, he began to develop a reputation for integrity. Moreover, he was intelligent enough to surround himself with men and women who, far from being lackeys, made up a dynamic team.

The first issues René Lévesque had to deal with concerned Noranda Mines. For a long time, the Quebec subsoil had been a natural resource that the Americans had exploited due to the complacency of Union Nationale premier, Maurice Duplessis. Lévesque laid out the numbers: the government had wasted the province's profits; the deficits were increas-ing. "It's scandalous!"

On top of that, during the trips to Rouyn-Noranda, Lévesque discovered that the administrators of the mine were all unilingual anglophones. In one of his inimitable impetuous outbursts, he spoke of "white Rhodesians" of Noranda. He denounced the intoler-ance and contempt of the leaders of the large-scale mining organizations. In Cabinet, Lévesque proposed that the State become involved in managing Quebec's natural resources. "We have young engineers who've left here due to a lack of work. They should come back." With this rationale in mind, Jean Lesage's gov-ernment of the early sixties created several Crown cor-porations whose acronyms would become instantly recognized, such as SOQUEM (Quebec Mining Exploration Company) and SGF (General Investment

Corporation), institutions that indicated the rise of a welfare state, which would be one of the overriding characteristics of the Quiet Revolution. For the upcoming generation of francophones, it was above all an opportunity to find a steady job in the public service.

But presenting new ideas to a Liberal government growing accustomed to power was never easy; over time, Lévesque lost his illusions and isolated himself from his colleagues, who found him intrusive. He wanted too much. He went too fast. His next battle would make waves – or rather, sparks: the nationalization of electricity.

⌒

"Tell me if it can be done and how much it's likely to cost us."

In his home on Woodbury Avenue, Lévesque handed a thick file over to Jacques Parizeau, an economist and professor. The latter wished he'd had more time to analyse the document in detail.

"At first glance, nationalizing electrical companies appears feasible to me."

The blue book was a plan to develop a hydroelectric network that could well become the flagship of the Quebec economy. At a recent caucus, Lévesque had tried to sell his project: the most mistrustful ministers had disagreed openly. What debt would the government have to incur to buy what at first glance seemed a white elephant? Lévesque was presenting the nationalization of electricity as a fait accompli. What exactly was his goal? He wanted the government to buy up the various private companies so that Hydro-Québec, which had been operating since the forties, would become the sole producer and distributor of electricity! Lévesque was alone in his quest and many resented him.

"Quebec is a millionaire," he said, lighting another cigarette, "but from all this wealth we derive but a pittance."

According to Parizeau, such an undertaking would cost over five million dollars, a third of the government budget! They had to come up with the money. And the money they needed was in the States. So what? New York was only about two hours from Montreal.

∞

Fifty kilometres from Quebec City, Lac à l'Épaule was a haven in the hollow of the Parc des Laurentides. There, at the beginning of September, Jean Lesage gathered his cabinet for a two-day retreat. Discussion would become heated. Lévesque took to the road telling himself he would go for broke. His final words to his secretary were "put my things in order!" If things did go badly, he was ready to vacate his office.

The first day, the atmosphere was convivial; Jean Lesage, already at the bar, warmly greeted his ministers. The real confrontation would occur the next afternoon. Everyone knew that nationalization of electricity would be discussed. Lévesque had barely two or three allies. In order to have his project accepted, he had to convince those with no opinion, those afraid to take a stand, and the yes-men who would side with the leader.

They wanted numbers! Lévesque provided them without hesitating, for he had an excellent grasp of his subject. He told them that the American market was ready to provide three hundred million, or half of the cost of amalgamating the eleven private companies managing Quebec's hydroelectric assets. Those present gasped in surprise: such a financial transaction seemed enormous. People voiced their opposition to Lévesque's enthusiasm. Georges Marler attacked him directly, resenting the way he had grabbed the spotlight and his socialist ideas. Things became unpleasant.

"We are headed straight for bankruptcy. What do we have against the management of Shawinigan Power?"

Throughout the entire debate, seated at the head of the table, Premier Lesage remained silent. Then, with a conspiratorial glance at Georges-Émile Lapalme, he began:

"What would you say to an immediate election?"

Combining an election with the plan to nationalize electricity took nerve! The Liberal government would thus run for office after only two years in power, well before the end of their mandate! René Lévesque, who hadn't imagined this possibility, was thrilled. This time, he would have a real plan to defend when he campaigned – a worthy challenge.

Without giving his ministers time to recover from their surprise, Lesage added:

"I'm thinking of calling it for November 14."

The Liberals had three months to carry off a victory, to show that their party's rise to power in 1960 had been no mere accident.

∞

Once the upcoming election was announced, René Lévesque took to the roads of Quebec. As the rural counties were Union Nationale strongholds, he made sure to visit all regions. Taking with him a film recreating the times of *Point de mire*, the Minister of Natural Resources recalled the period when he had been a television star. He met with immediate success as he repeated: "It is inconceivable that 95 per cent of the Quebec population controls but 10 per cent of its economy." His nationalism was instinctive. Taking possession of hydroelectric resources was the first action leading to political emancipation.

With their slogan *Maintenant ou jamais: Maîtres chez nous* (Now or never: masters in our own house), the Liberals were re-elected on November 14, 1962. Jean Lesage's campaign was successful almost across the board. Only three days before heading to the polls, Lesage crushed rival Daniel Johnson in a first televised debate. Like John F. Kennedy, who had rid himself of Richard Nixon on CBS in 1960, the leader of the Liberal Party shone on the Radio-Canada telecast. From then on, television became the medium that mattered for carrying off a victory. For René Lévesque, it was simply another means of communication – one he mastered effortlessly.

∞

The Liberals' second mandate began with the hope of change after two years in power. The creation of new departments, such as Education, marked the continuation of the Quiet Revolution. Other legislation consolidated the rise of francophones. But a whole generation that had been suppressed began to make demands, frustrated with the status quo. Francophones, a majority in Quebec, could no longer tolerate the disregard for their culture. A new social class was denouncing injustice and demanding jobs in decision-making positions. In response to the crisis in Quebec, in 1963 Prime Minister Lester Pearson appointed a royal commission, the Laurendeau-Dunton Commission on Bilingualism and Biculturalism.

For the first time since the Rebellion of 1837, the country's stability was being threatened, and violence became a tool used to promote ideas and provoke change. In this highly charged atmosphere, bombs exploded in Westmount. In 1963, the Front de Libération du Québec entered history; with three consonants the FLQ put its stamp on this new page.

Until the mid-sixties, René Lévesque had been virtually uninterested in constitutional questions. Asked by an anglophone newspaper, however, he stated that Canada was made up of two nations, not ten provinces. The man who described himself as "a native" when travelling outside Quebec remained convinced that Canadian Confederation allowed Quebecers to be emancipated. He opposed those who were preparing to found the Rassemblement pour l'indépendance nationale (RIN). With a ram's head as its logo, the RIN was a political party that openly advocated Quebec independence and planned on running candidates in the next election.

René Lévesque continued to work within the
Liberal Party, but his heart was no longer in it. Ever
since electricity had been nationalized, his enthusiasm
had waned, and he felt as if he were going around in
circles. This second mandate was looking more difficult
than imagined. The Liberal dream team had run out of
steam. Rivalry broke out. Lévesque was often criticized: his star status irritated people. Jean Lesage,
guessing that the member from Laurier was thinking of
resigning, reshuffled his cabinet in October 1965 and
named Lévesque Minister of Family and Social
Services. So much for economics – from now on the
black sheep would have to deal with social problems –
of which there were many. At that time, the department's files reported mothers in need and crèches for
abandoned infants, and the vocabulary used evoked an
antiquated mentality, a time when the clergy gave alms
and provided charity to the poor.

"We have to eliminate private charity," announced
the newcomer.

With his reforms against under-education and
making outcasts of people on the fringes of society,
René Lévesque saw the department, which he had
once called that of "old age," in a new light. He discovered, in particular, the extent of social misery existing
in Quebec despite the extensive cleanup his government had announced. Eric Kierans in Health and
Lévesque in Family and Social Services worked
together to meet growing economic requirements:
increase monthly allowances to families in need,
promise a free health-insurance regime for the poor.
The other ministers fumed. In conflict with Ottawa

over the federal pension plan, Lévesque provoked friction. His colleagues accused him of being a Quebec nationalist, but his stubbornness proved effective. Quebec ended up establishing its own pension plan and launched the Caisse de dépôt et placement. Meanwhile, Jean Lesage, concerned about the climate within the party, had only one choice: call an election. It would be held June 5, 1966.

∞

"I had just set foot in Bermuda when I received a telegram: Lesage was asking me to go see him in Florida, to tell me that we were going back on the campaign trail!"

Angry at not having been able to see all his promised social reforms through, Lévesque had no illusion as to the outcome of this election. Daniel Johnson's arrival as leader of the Union Nationale had changed the Quebec political scene: with his book *Égalité ou indépendance* (Equality or Independence), published in 1965, the new leader of the blues, the Union Nationale, obliged Liberals, the reds, to redefine their constitutional position, forcing them to move closer to Ottawa. This did little to win over Lévesque. In any case, he had lost his passion; the Liberal Party had been only a way for him to put forward progressive ideas. Bitter, grumpy, he campaigned in his Laurier riding, which he easily won. On the evening of June 5, the results came in: the Liberals had been beaten, even though their percentage of votes surpassed that of the Union Nationale, who were elected.

In the Opposition! Lévesque couldn't imagine himself criticizing Daniel Johnson's ministers. Could he be content with half-measures after having known the exhilaration of power?

7

Breaking Through the Wall of Fear

The defeat in the provincial election had hurt the Liberals; resentment was simmering. People sought to lay blame. René Lévesque, aloof, organized retreats. He wanted to know what his friends thought about Quebec independence. Two political parties, the Rassemblement pour l'indépendance nationale and the Ralliement national, had gathered almost 10 per cent of votes in June 1966. For how much longer could they ignore this phenomenon that a majority of the younger generation supported? While Jean Marchand, Gérard Pelletier, and Pierre Trudeau, the three doves, may have wanted to impose a francophone presence in the House of Commons in Ottawa, dissatisfaction with the federal government was increasing.

October 1970: invocation of the War Measures Act.
The army is in Montreal.

Lévesque savagely stubbed out another cigarette into the already-full ashtray. Was he interested in moving over to the feds? No, he replied to his circle of friends at the Saint-Denis Club:

"When I was a journalist, I travelled across the country from coast to coast; I know Canada only too well, and I never felt at home there."

Dissatisfied with the work of the Liberals in Quebec, deeming it useless to fight in Ottawa, what did he want? One event triggered a change of direction. In July 1967, General de Gaulle, from atop Montreal City Hall, shouted "Vive le Québec libre!": the words were both resounding and disturbing.

"As I was walking down the street back to my car," he would later say, "I saw people shouting '*Independence – Yes! De Gaulle said so!*'" I told myself that we didn't need someone else to come here and tell us what to do. If we want Quebec's independence, we're the ones who'll make it happen."

It is time to act, he thought. The next Liberal convention, planned for three months hence, would be decisive.

∽

After the manifesto *Pour un Québec souverain dans une nouvelle union canadienne* (For a Sovereign Quebec in a New Canadian Union) appeared in *Le Devoir*, René Lévesque was perceived as a crypto-separatist. At the Château Frontenac, a revolt was organized against him. Jean Lesage, who had never hidden his unfailing support of federalism, was clearly a part of it. The first day of the convention, delegates agreed on the majority of points in the Liberal platform. When the constitutional question arose, the discussions turned sour. On Friday, October 13, as supporters gathered in the hotel ballroom, René Lévesque learned that procedure had just been changed. For resolutions regarding the status of Quebec, the vote would be done by raising of hands, not by secret ballot. Would supporters be brave enough to follow the man who would propose to the Liberals assembled the change in direction approved by his riding on September 18? That day, René Lévesque had suggested voting for Quebec sovereignty within the framework of an economic association with Canada. He had stated: "This adventure is our opportunity to get out of the 'madhouse' of Canadian Confederation." But he was not naive. Around him, hostility was growing. The "member from Laurier," as he was now called, had fallen from grace.

It was a case of the fox in the henhouse.

Lévesque and his approximately twenty supporters listened to Jean Lesage's speech. The tone was bombastic, the words condemning outright "people who want to isolate us on a desert isle: with them we would likely be cut off, without communication with the rest of the world."

Lévesque couldn't take it any longer. As he rose and left, muttering could be heard in the room. There was no longer any doubt; they wanted him to leave. His opponents were plotting against him, saying that the fiery idealist would be less dangerous outside the party. Former friends, ministers in Ottawa, had come up with a scheme for doing so, but Lévesque ignored the rumours. He would return the afternoon of the next day. To win.

On Saturday, October 14, the room was packed. Seeing the member from Laurier enter, delegates cried: "Out with Lévesque! Out with Lévesque!" When he took the microphone, Liberals were divided; it seemed as if the majority didn't want to follow him. Lévesque used metaphors, tried to make people understand he didn't want to destroy the country. They had to break through the wall of fear. He spoke of "two semi-detached houses." He used words like "independence" and "interdependence." It was too much! For four hours, debates were fast and furious. Personal attacks came from all sides. It was almost six p.m. when Lévesque asked for a final right of reply. He threw in the towel: it was now clear he would resign. Voicing his intent, he expressed one regret:

"It isn't easy to leave a party you have worked in for seven years."

Around him, people rose, applauding his courage. René Lévesque left the room to the cheers of his supporters. Others booed him.

From that moment on, he would fight for Quebec sovereignty.

∞

He was leaving the Liberal Party, but René Lévesque had no intention of leaving politics. In Montreal in mid-November, four hundred delegates outlined the plan for a movement to unite sovereigntist forces.

What name should they choose? Among nineteen, they selected Mouvement souveraineté-association (MSA), or Sovereignty-Association Movement. Lévesque was perplexed; he would have preferred Parti Souverainiste or Sovereigntist Party. The MSA was merely a starting point; they had to hold an official founding conference if they wanted to be taken seriously. Meanwhile, the member from Laurier continued his crusade. On January 17, 1968, he launched *Option Québec* at the Prince-Charles Restaurant. Fifty thousand copies sold in a few weeks. In April, at the Maurice Richard Arena, the general meeting was only a partial success: they became mired down in pointless discussions that prevented transforming the MSA into a political party. From the start, radicals and moderates were at loggerheads. The most contentious issue was anglophone rights. Lévesque determined that one of the most difficult tasks consisted of reconciling both antagonistic currents. Meanwhile, political pressure at the federal level was on the rise. At the end of the convention, a friend took him aside:

"Have you seen what's happening in Ottawa?"

"I'm not worried," he replied, with just enough seriousness that people inferred he was nevertheless somewhat worried.

On April 20, 1968, while sovereigntist supporters were betting on their future, Pierre Trudeau succeeded Lester B. Pearson as leader of the Liberal Party of Canada. Trudeau and Lévesque were rivals, each with his own national dream. For twenty years, they would cross paths. But at present, with Trudeau in Ottawa and the federal election called for the end of June,

René Lévesque's game plan had been disrupted; now he also had to defeat the radical wing of his party, who preferred RIN leader Pierre Bourgault over him. Time was running out: only something unforeseen could help Lévesque.

∞

On June 24, 1968, Pierre Trudeau agreed to attend Saint-Jean-Baptiste Day celebrations. "You have to back out," he was told, "the separatists are just waiting for the opportunity to attack you. And you won't be safe." But the leader of the Liberal Party of Canada dismissed this advice. Prior to his election as Canada's head of state, wouldn't this be a fine chance to show the rest of the country that he was unafraid of the sovereigntists?

Pierre Trudeau, among the who's who of personalities appearing on the grandstand in front of the Montreal Public Library, leaned forward to watch the parade marching up Sherbrooke Street. After the bugle bands came the floats. But bit by bit, the tension was mounting. What was going on? Shouting could be heard from Lafontaine Park. Police officers awaited the signal to charge into the crowd. A projectile was thrown. Confrontation was inevitable. Guests rose and tried desperately to force Pierre Trudeau to leave, but he resisted, and sat down again. The Saint-Jean-Baptiste parade was turning into bedlam, what with majorettes fleeing and families running in all directions. Police officers, armed with riot batons, seized about a hundred demonstrators. Among the culprits slammed into the paddy wagons was Pierre Bourgault, leader of the Rassemblement pour l'indépendance nationale.

"This violence was useless. All it did was help Pierre Trudeau get elected prime minister of Canada, and by an overwhelming majority," commented René Lévesque in the days that followed.

He was displeased by the hint of scandal surrounding the RIN, for he had always wanted to unite sovereigntist forces. While the threesome (the RIN, RN and MSA) at first glance seemed unlikely, Lévesque agreed to compromises so that they could band together: "I have no problem with Gilles Grégoire of the Ralliement national (RN), but Pierre Bourgault is another story." Above all he sought to clearly differentiate himself from all those impatient to achieve Quebec independence at any cost. As the head of the RIN had been seized on that crazy June 24, Lévesque could now run as sole leader of the sovereigntist forces.

On October 14, 1968, at Quebec City's Petit Colisée, about a thousand delegates adopted the platform of a new political party to be called the Parti Québécois, a name suggested by Gilles Grégoire that René Lévesque didn't like. Its logo, on the other hand, received unanimous approval. Designed by painter and poet Roland Giguère, the blue circle with a red tip cutting into its core symbolized national unity.

Carried to the podium by dozens of supporters, René Lévesque, whom people had predicted would lose scarcely one year earlier, was at the dawn of a new political career. Things were going well and he was in love. He wrote to Corinne Côté: "I hope this doesn't sound ridiculous. I am consumed by an overwhelming (but very respectful) need to see you."

Tender feelings had surfaced: his heart was no longer his own.

∞

Then a society in transition, Quebec was dozing on a smouldering volcano. The linguistic crisis would awaken it. In September, in Saint-Léonard, a northern suburb of Montreal, francophone parents criticized the massive integration of immigrants to English schools. Demonstrations increased and the discontented took to the streets. They accused the Union Nationale government of being spineless. Since the death of Daniel Johnson, the day before the opening of the Manic dam, in September 1968, the Union Nationale had been losing ground. Jean-Jacques Bertrand lacked the polish of his predecessor. The language laws put forth by his Department of Education quickly poured oil on the flames. On October 23, 1969, a final project was presented to the members of the National Assembly: Bill 63, whose Section 2 ensured parents free choice of the language of instruction, giving English legal status equal to French. Voices were raised. This bill was a disgrace! Opposition groups brandishing the threat of assimilation were formed outside Parliament. At first sympathetic to the government, whom he felt had the courage to attack the problem head on, René Lévesque, an independent member since leaving the ranks of the Liberals, little by little distanced himself from the views expressed by the Union Nationale. Actually, this conflict caught him off guard. It was clear, however, that he would not side with the radicals. He wished to emphasize that the Parti Québécois had not been founded against the anglophones. Behind this stance, his desire to become the leader of all Quebecers one day began to take shape.

Amid this restlessness, Lévesque achieved quite a coup by recruiting Jacques Parizeau, who joined the PQ in 1969. A professor at the École des hautes études commerciales, the economist would permanently influence PQ ideology. More to the left than Lévesque, he presented a paradox of respectability and audacity. Following Parizeau's advice, Member Lévesque criticized in the House Bill 63's "intellectually dishonest fabrication." For the present, Lévesque was suggesting limiting the rights of anglophones to their actual numbers, which would prevent immigrants from enrolling their children in English schools. But he no longer had any doubt that only the sovereignty of Quebec could settle the linguistic issue.

In the next provincial election, what could Lévesque hope for? Polls showed that 30 per cent of francophones supported his party. Perhaps the PQ was on a roll, but a new Liberal leader who'd arrived was now transforming the political playing field. In politics, like in blackjack, chance often had unpleasant surprises in store.

∞

A stern-looking economist with dark glasses and neatly combed hair, Robert Bourassa was the man who was needed. In 1970, Quebec was talking about jobs. The young Harvard graduate promised a hundred thousand of them. On April 29, voters reacted favourably to his message: heading up seventy-two Liberal members, he would form the new government. Although the Péquistes were happy at having elected seven members representing the sovereigntist option, they were nevertheless disappointed with the results. Coming fourth in the number of seats did not reflect their 23 per cent of the vote. The Union Nationale, elected by less of a majority, nevertheless elected seventeen members and made up the official Opposition. At the Paul Sauvé Centre, René Lévesque, who had lost in his own county of Laurier, rose to the podium.

"Doesn't this defeat look like a victory?"

Supporters were carried away with enthusiasm. They would have to work hard to achieve their goal, but there was hope. After all, four years wasn't so long to wait, considering the political party had only been born about twenty months earlier.

On October 5, 1970, Agence France-Presse released the following dispatch: at eight-thirty that morning, the British Trade Commissioner, James Richard Cross, was kidnapped by two masked men claiming to represent the Front de libération du Québec. Events that occurred elsewhere in the world, in places like Bolivia and Argentina, were now happening here, in Westmount, a well-to-do area of Montreal. The letters FLQ conjured up images of the sixties, of bombs ripping apart mailboxes. Now they heralded one of the worst crises ever faced by the country. René Lévesque immediately condemned the kidnapping of James Richard Cross. He feared opponents of the FLQ and PQ would maliciously lump the two of them together. Indeed, while a similar goal existed behind both initialisms, the means for achieving independence differed radically from one to the other. "I have always rejected violence; which inevitably leads to repression," René Lévesque mentioned to journalists at a briefing. Lending his support to the Quebec premier, he suggested negotiating, a stance he would maintain throughout the October Crisis.

Elected barely six months previously, the Bourassa government was powerless. A hunt for communiqués began in an attempt to uncover the abductors. Journalists emptied garbage cans and roamed lobbies and corridors of downtown buildings to find messages from the FLQ. The first days were almost farcical. FLQ members demanded the liberation of political prisoners, safe conduct, money, and the reading of a manifesto. In Ottawa, Prime Minister Pierre Trudeau set up a crisis centre. Discussions were firm, then wavered. Should they yield to the kidnappers' demands? What about agreeing to the last demand? At first glance, reading a pamphlet seemed harmless enough.

On Thursday, October 8, at ten-thirty at night, the FLQ manifesto was read on Radio-Canada. In fifteen minutes, the text – full of vitriol and outrageous distortion – attacked the country's political authorities and demanded socio-economic changes. The passage in which the Liberation cell wrote: "For a moment we believed it was worth channelling our energies, our impatience, as René Lévesque says, in the Parti Québécois," angered the leader of the Party. Directly targeted by this excerpt, he responded to journalists saying it would be treacherous to confuse his party with rebels advocating unrest. To put an end to the gossip, he signed an act of faith in democracy in the *Journal de Montréal*, where he had been hired after his defeat in April 1970.

The reading of the FLQ manifesto exacerbated the conflict, which, far from being resolved, took an unexpected turn. Away from the National Assembly, where he was not sitting, Lévesque feared above all that the Quebec government would be reduced to asking Ottawa to settle this crisis.

James Richard Cross had been kidnapped five days earlier. He was sequestered in an undisclosed location. Efforts to locate him seemed in vain; desperately, people hunted for comminiqués from the FLQ featuring the silhouette of an 1837 patriot. The weekend got off to a difficult start, with reversals straight out of a detective novel. On Friday, October 8, René Lévesque travelled to Lac Achigan to relax for a couple of days at his friend Marc Brière's place. After a game of tennis, he went back into the cottage. On television, the Minister of Justice was reading a text. They turned up the volume and felt caught up in a nightmare! Jérôme Choquette officially announced the news that Pierre

Laporte, Minister of Labour and Immigration, standing in front of his St. Lambert home, had just been kidnapped by masked men armed with machine-guns. The government was struck speechless. How far would the crisis go? For Lévesque, there was a personal connection to the tragedy.

"I knew Laporte when we were both in the Liberal Party, with Lesage."

Today, more than ever, he felt a bond with the former colleague whose life was in danger.

As leader of an opposition party not elected to the National Assembly, Lévesque felt it was not his role to interfere in this crisis, nor should he provoke or criticize. He watched the goings-on in the Bourassa government, telling himself he would intervene only if asked for advice.

Laporte's first sign of life was a harrowing letter that made the front page of special editions of newspapers. The writing was hesitant, as if his hand had been trembling in fear: "Sunday, 3 p.m. I believe I am writing the most significant letter of my life."

In seven points, the minister insisted that the police call off their searches. He begged the man he addressed as *Monsieur Robert Bourassa*, beginning the letter *My dear Robert*. Then, in the last paragraph, a harrowing appeal: "Decide on my life or my death. I am counting on you, and thank you."

An hour later, the premier refused to give in to blackmail and answered that "governing involves making choices." From then on, Robert Bourassa would have to live with the choice he had made of his own free will.

∞

For days, the government was at bay; the dialogue between the authorities and FLQ members was leading nowhere. Things looked grim. The day before Thanksgiving, Claude Ryan, editor of *Le Devoir*, received a phone call. It was René Lévesque. The two men had rarely shared the same opinions, but the leader of the Parti Québécois was now grateful for the moderate tone of the newspaper's editorials.

"I've heard that something serious is about to happen. We should convene people like us who see eye to eye and whose opinion carries weight when it comes to making decisions. I suggest you organize a common front to encourage Bourassa to negotiate and especially to prevent the feds from meddling in all this."

Less than twenty-four hours later, sixteen opinion leaders met at the Holiday Inn in Montreal. Lévesque withdrew into a room to be alone. In less than an hour, he wrote a text they all would have to approve. At the press conference, René Lévesque reaffirmed unwavering support for the Liberal government. The declaration of the signatories boiled down to four points: the life of the two hostages took precedence over any other concern; they had to negotiate their exchange for that of the political prisoners; the FLQ represented only a minority of revolutionaries; the Quebec government alone had to find a solution to this crisis.

Everything happened at once. The group organized by Lévesque had the idea of setting up a parallel government – a notion which gained ground. At the Queen Elizabeth Hotel, Premier Bourassa had to make a decision as quickly as possible. His image weakened with each passing moment of hesitation. On October 15, he called an emergency meeting of the National Assembly, not to settle the crisis, but to vote on an anti-strike law against medical specialists, for in the meantime, the social climate had deteriorated.

It was time to act.

In the night, Prime Minister Trudeau invoked the War Measures Act. Having come into force during the First World War, this law suspended *habeas corpus* and abolished civil liberties. Upon the slightest suspicion, anyone could be declared guilty of terrorism or of wanting to overthrow the government. At four o'clock in the morning, soldiers entered Montreal to ensure public safety. They began arresting people and conducting searches.

Lévesque claimed "all hell had broken loose"; the words stigmatized a country in disarray. "Quebec no longer has a government," he wrote in the *Journal de Montréal*. On October 16, he submitted a text wherein he implored the government to negotiate in order to save the lives of the two hostages. He didn't know if James Richard Cross was alive, nor did he know what had happened to Pierre Laporte.

∞

At CKAC radio in Montreal, the third anonymous call of the day had just come in. Should it be taken seriously? The voice was insistent: "You will find a communiqué in the lobby of Port Royal Theatre at Place des Arts." There, precise instructions were provided, specifying a road to take, leading to the St. Hubert Airport. About a hundred feet from the fence that surrounded a military aircraft plant, a car was parked – the one used to abduct Pierre Laporte. It was eleven-thirty at night. Specialists from the Canadian army had no trouble opening the trunk of the green Chevrolet: the Minister's hunched-up body was wrapped in a blanket, head resting on a pillow, wrists bloodied. The man had been assassinated.

∞

At Parti Québécois headquarters on Christophe-Colomb, René Lévesque gave free rein to his emotions. He wept. Forty-eight years old – Pierre Laporte and he were the same age. Memories resurfaced, happy moments they'd shared in the Liberal Party in the early sixties. It was all so long ago.

On those rare occasions when the emotional floodgates opened, a song would come back to him: it was Léo Ferré singing words written by the French medieval poet Rutebeuf: "Que sont mes amis devenus... ce sont amis que vent emporte" / What has become of my friends... these are friends the wind has carried away. Returning to his Pine Avenue apartment, Lévesque quickened his step. As he walked through a park in the darkness, he was surprised to discover he was afraid.

∞

Where was James Cross? Was he still alive? It was as if Pierre Laporte's death had marked the expected end of the tragedy: the events of the October Crisis no longer made media headlines. Despite continual police searching since the invocation of the War Measures Act, the culprits were still on the loose. Life went on.

A columnist at the *Journal de Montréal*, Lévesque set aside news of the crisis and instead attacked the policies of the Bourassa government. What were the Liberals doing for highways, for employment, for housing? The true leader of the Opposition, he ordered: "Admit your mistakes."

Then, as if in a bad thriller, new developments began to proliferate in the October Crisis. In December policemen put in place the last pieces of the puzzle. They discovered a house in St. Hubert and a room in which the windows had been barred. There, over a seven-day period, Pierre Laporte had prayed to be set free. The FLQ members who had assassinated the Liberal minister were soon arrested, then imprisoned. James Richard Cross was finally found in a Montreal North apartment. His abductors were given safe passage to Cuba.

The October Crisis ended as it began: an ember that flared up with lightning speed and left a terrible scar.

The events of the autumn were a hard blow for the PQ. At the bottom of the polls, René Lévesque needed to rise in popularity if he didn't want the journey begun three years earlier to have been but an interlude in Quebec political history.

8

The Moment of Truth

Heavy losses. Afraid of being kept on file by the police, several party supporters did not renew their PQ membership. The departure of ten thousand members reduced income by 75 per cent. The October Crisis had left a heavy toll. For a while, René Lévesque wondered whether he should remain. If he left, he would be proving the federalists right. And he hadn't said his last word. The announcement that he would have an opponent for the Parti Québécois leadership spurred him on: things would heat up at the next national convention.

In February 1971, about a thousand delegates met at the Patro Roc Amadour community centre in

René Lévesque at the Paul Sauvé Centre on October 29, 1973, election night.

Quebec City. Taking stock of their situation provided an opportunity to heal the wounds of the post-October period. The party's now radical leanings disturbed René Lévesque, who had difficulty accepting Pierre Bourgault's election to the executive. Running for leader of the Parti Québécois, André Larocque put up an honest fight – a minority of delegates supported him – but there was no real suspense. The PQ leader was re-elected as head of his party.

With the ordeal of the convention out of the way, other obstacles arose. As Lévesque had not sat in the National Assembly since his personal defeat in April, he had trouble steering a party whose moods were unpredictable. The seven elected members criticized his attitude: "You're leaving us on our own in Quebec City! You never come to our meetings." But what could he accomplish in the capital? Lévesque had never been comfortable in the Opposition: power alone interested him. After a short time in purgatory, his party was energized in 1972 when Claude Morin joined. Deputy Minister of Intergovernmental Affairs since 1963, Morin was welcomed into the PQ. Lévesque quickly gave him star billing. He both trusted and liked him. "Because he's less complicated than Jacques Parizeau." And Morin was a phenomenal card player.

∽

"What a great idea!"

Initially, he had hesitated. Wouldn't this detour by means of a referendum kill Article I of the PQ, which had the goal of achieving Quebec sovereignty? In 1972,

Lévesque was listening to Claude Morin, who assured him that they needed to create a distinction between the Parti Québécois' accession to power and Quebec's accession to sovereignty. His game plan was realistic:

"First, we get elected. Then, we hold a referendum to ask the people for the right to negotiate sovereignty-association."

"At the next national convention," replied Lévesque, "you are the one who'll defend the resolution to members. Then we'll find out what they think."

Since the founding of the party in 1968, all PQ meetings had led to confrontation between the orthodox members and the extremists. This time, the imprisonment of three union leaders by the Liberal government inflamed discussions and widened the gap between the radicals and those who chose to remain neutral.

"The unions are our allies," certain delegates proclaimed. "We must vote to free the leaders of the central labour bodies and denounce the Liberal government."

The sooner this convention ends the better! thought Lévesque, trapped in what felt like a rat race. He couldn't stand being portrayed as a reactionary by the left wing. His authority vacillated when people rejected the idea of a referendum despite his public support of Claude Morin's resolution. On the other hand, Pierre Bourgault's leaving the executive of the party seemed a good omen. "One less person to watch out for!" He was suspicious of any excess that could adversely affect his image as a unifier. When supporters spoke to him of founding a political party to advocate

Quebec sovereignty on the federal scene, his response was definitive:

"Never!"

His battlefield did not extend beyond borders. No question of confronting Ottawa's Liberals, who, since Wilfrid Laurier, had won the majority of Quebec ridings hands down.

"Did you see Trudeau on October 30? Without Quebec, he would have lost. We simply cannot weigh ourselves down with another political structure; we have enough problems as it is."

∞

Kept in the opposition in the National Assembly, the PQ was able to meet up as a family at conventions. In February 1973 Lévesque warned his supporters to ready themselves as an election was fast approaching. But the Parti Québécois, seeking an identity, was divided. The most acerbic criticism came from the seven members who travelled back and forth between Montreal and Quebec City. "You have no idea what parliamentary work involves!" they reproached him. Lévesque was no longer even thinking about taking office, he just wanted to avoid divisiveness so the PQ could one day form the official Opposition.

At the end of September, as the election campaign began, the PQ was ill-prepared. Forced to close ranks, inept, they didn't have enough time to regain control. On October 29, the Liberal Party swept to victory: Robert Bourassa was re-elected with two hundred members and almost 55 per cent of the popular vote.

The phenomenon of the young economist who looked like an eternal student worked to the hilt. Quebecers liked the reassuring image he projected. The Péquistes now had only six members. Although they'd gained an additional 7 per cent of voters, they nevertheless had lost a seat in the National Assembly – a real disappointment. The reds carried former political parties that were the Union Nationale and the Parti Créditiste along in their wake; their sweep redesigned the political landscape. In the PQ, the most optimistic rejoiced at being in the official Opposition in Quebec City. Choices were clearer. In the next election, sovereignty would become an alternative to the constitutional status quo. For that to happen, they would have to sit tight for another four years.

Driven by this resurgence of hope, René Lévesque entered the Paul Sauvé Centre to applause, cries, and tears. For the second time, he would not sit in the Assembly; he had been defeated by a Liberal in Dorion. The Parti Québécois leader stepped up to the podium. In 1970, he had said that the defeat looked like a victory. On October 29, 1973 he spoke of a "moral victory," another expression he had found to buoy up his supporters. And it worked. Once again, he rallied his flock. In adversity, René Lévesque had the knack of breathing life back into dying embers.

But the defeats were piling up, becoming increasingly difficult to bear. The next election would be the ultimate test. "I may leave beforehand," he admitted to journalists.

Like everyone else, he wanted to live a little. His savings were down to nothing, and the separation from his wife was costing him a lot. He was not a member of the National Assembly, so his column at the *Journal de Montréal* was his only source of income. Everything would be easier should he decide to return to work in the media. Hadn't he been a television star before entering politics? He sought a way out; his friends had trouble holding him back. *After all, he's the right man for the job*, they told themselves, *we still need him. There's no one now who can replace him.*

⌒

Forming an effective Opposition with only six PQ members was difficult.

"We could found our own newspaper!"

It started out as a thrilling venture. The first issue of *Le Jour* appeared in February 1974. Thirty thousand copies were printed in the first few months, but then the problems began. René Lévesque sensed the same rebellious mood that had characterized the 1960s student protests: they were becoming bogged down in demands, veering off-course, and drifting into anarchy. Managing a newspaper seemed to him the wrong direction to take. And he could no longer bear to see *Le Jour* oppose his ideas. Nothing exasperates a leader more than to discover his most bitter adversaries inside his own party. *Le Jour* was biting the hand that fed it. This was too much for Lévesque.

At the end of the 1974 convention, during which the plan to hold a referendum for Quebec to accede to sovereignty ended up being passed, the Parti Québécois looked in good shape for the next election.

Reassured by polls indicating that the PQ was making headway with francophones, the leader wanted no more impediments to their progress. He distanced himself from the dissension at *Le Jour* and openly suggested closing down the sovereigntist newspaper. It was simply a question of salary; the drop in circulation indicated that they could now close the chapter on this project born in enthusiasm and hope. That interlude was over. Once again, Lévesque had managed to bring the agitators under control. He had disciplined them without looking like a tyrant.

∞

"People who claim they can lead Quebec but can't even run a poor little newspaper!"

With a derisive laugh, Robert Bourassa thought he had scored a point. On the air at CKAC, he was confronting René Lévesque, who knew how to fight back, and retaliated:

"People who can't run the Reform Club, and what's worse, have just placed it in bankruptcy – for your information, people could find that even more disturbing!"

Touché! In this election campaign, the gloves were coming off. Lévesque, encouraged by his progress in the polls, moved to the foreground. Moreover, the concept of changeover between political parties made it seem likely that the first party to advocate Quebec sovereignty could be elected. The more pessimistic warned against counting chickens. After all, didn't the Liberals have the support of about twenty safe anglophone ridings? Lévesque remained confident. In meetings, he received a hero's greeting. He was given the riding of Taillon on the South Shore so he would finally have a seat in the Quebec legislature. During the thirty-day campaign, the PQ had the wind in their sails. With no storm on the horizon, they were headed for what scarcely ten years earlier had seemed impossible when René Lévesque, leading up a few loyal friends, had left the Liberal Party to found the Parti Québécois.

On November 15, Quebecers awaited the results of the polls. This was no ordinary election. There was more nervousness and excitement in the air. At twenty minutes after eight, on public television, the camera focused on host Bernard Derome.

"If the trend holds, Radio-Canada predicts that…"

He paused for a second, before adding: "the Parti Québécois will lead the next government."

For the PQ supporters gathered at the Paul Sauvé Centre, the joy was overwhelming. They thought they were dreaming. It was too good to be true. On a giant screen, the results came in one by one, the ridings adding up: fifty, sixty-six, the final count reached seventy-one seats and 41 per cent of the popular vote. People were shouting! They wanted this happy evening to go on forever. On stage, hosts invited the crowd to dance and sing. The elected members appeared on the podium. And in Taillon? What had happened? People feared the worst. But this time, no problem! René Lévesque had been elected.

René Lévesque became premier of Quebec.

At the end of the evening, under photographers' flashbulbs, he arrived, cigarette between his lips. He made his way through supporters, hands touching him as he advanced. Embarrassed by this effusiveness, the orgy of lights and shouting, he grimaced, then smiled. On the podium, his friends surrounded him, hugging him and crying. He walked to the microphone and the crowd at the Paul Sauvé Centre fell silent. His words, choked with emotion, imprinted themselves in people's memories. He spoke in his inimitable way; detachedly, and despite a hint of nonchalance, resoundingly.

"I never thought I would be so proud to be a Quebecer! We are not a small people, we are perhaps something like a great people."

The cheers and songs marked the grand finale on November 15, 1976. But for the sovereigntists, their dream was still a long way off.

∞

The PQ government, which claimed to adhere to a social democratic program, undertook major reforms in culture, economics, and politics. Its first two pieces of legislation would make their mark: the Charter of the French Language acknowledging francophones' majority status, and the law on political party financing, which placed Quebec at the forefront of western democracies. If René Lévesque encouraged his ministers to introduce daring projects, he did not forget that the PQ owed its victory to half the votes cast. Lévesque advised proceeding with care. Being one of the more experienced in the House, he was not afraid to curb the dangerous ambitions of the most headstrong.

Meanwhile, at each convention, the great family gathering, supporters worried:

"What about the referendum? When are we going to hold it?"

In October 1978, Lévesque announced that they had to make some adjustments. He was doing very poorly in the polls, and wondered if he shouldn't consider a third solution: abandoning the idea of sovereignty-association to demand the most political power possible from the feds. For the diehard sovereigntists, this was a giant step backwards.

Later, at the June convention, the PQ planned to hold a referendum to ask for a mandate to negotiate with Canada. They stated that the PQ government would not unilaterally declare Quebec sovereignty; if Ottawa refused to sit down with the PQ government, they would have to hold another referendum to ask voters to exercise the absolute rights of a sovereign state. "A scandal!" shouted the radicals. But René Lévesque liked this prudent approach. He thought that by asking for little, they would likely gain a lot.

One Wednesday morning, the PQ cabinet was meeting in the bunker. Clearly, the two factions were at loggerheads. Since Robert Burns had slammed the door on the government, the atmosphere had only deteriorated. The former Minister had declared to a Canadian Press journalist "I am convinced that the Parti Québécois will lose the referendum and don't want to be around when it happens." A real slap in the face. Lévesque was angry. He couldn't stand being told what to do. He was in no mood for threats.

"We are not opportunistic enough," certain people thought. "We need to take advantage of Pierre Trudeau's departure. It can't last long – the Conservative government is in the minority. With Joe Clark as prime minister of Canada, our chances are better."

Lévesque, however, told himself that an entire year remained before the end of the first PQ mandate – enough time to win a referendum.

∽

On December 19, 1979, the meeting began early in the morning; no one knew when it would end. The entire cabinet was present, for that day they were discussing how to word the referendum question. Lévesque, arriving late, sat down at the head of the table and lit a cigarette.

"We have two predicaments: poor Joe Clark, who has just been defeated in the House of Commons on a vote of confidence, and the Common Front, who are likely to throw a wrench in our plans."

With the Conservative leader gone, Trudeau's shadow loomed; he was the opponent the PQ didn't need. As for the public service, it had to be handled carefully. By temporarily suspending their right to strike and forcing union members to vote secretly, the PQ government had turned the majority of union members against them. But the sovereigntists needed the union members' vote. Timing was crucial, for the PQ were gambling on the political path they'd chosen. In the bunker, each of the ministers became acquainted with the basic structure of the referendum question they had prepared the day before. The two factions dividing the Parti Québécois had never been so far apart. Jacques Parizeau exploded: the preamble mentioned the possibility of a second referendum! Such a proposal had never been approved at the party convention. Lévesque listened. He remembered when Claude Morin had suggested this alternative to him. *It's a damn good idea,* he had thought at the time. Asking people for the right to negotiate, then coming back to voters with the results of these negotiations was democratic behaviour. But the caucus was split: the white paper entitled *La nouvelle entente Québec-Canada* (the new Quebec-Canada agreement) had not anticipated such a procedure. Several ministers would rather have seen a properly worded question. "It's only a rough draft," one grumbled, "we'll never agree on it!" The atmosphere was charged with ill feeling. The PQ leader asked each person to put forth his ideas. The approximately twenty people around the table tried to make themselves heard; they suggested various synonyms, stylistic devices, and punctuation. Irritable and impatient – he was wary of the acerbic integrationist wing – Lévesque jotted down notes on bits of paper.

Would they ever manage to word the question?

The most quarrelsome were angry that their leader hadn't involved them more closely in the drafting process. Most told themselves that this exercise in stylistics was useless. The die was cast. That evening, a quorum made up of a handful of caucus members ended up agreeing on the wording. Lévesque adjourned the meeting at three in the morning. Tomorrow would be an exceptional, historic day, journalists claimed. The setting: the National Assembly.

∞

His ministers applauded him. René Lévesque was riding high, confident in the success of his dream. Television cameras zoomed in on him. It was 3:17 p.m. when he began reading the question:

"The Government of Quebec has made public its proposal to negotiate a new agreement with the rest of Canada, based on the equality of nations; this agreement would enable Quebec to acquire exclusive power to make its laws, levy its taxes and establish relations abroad – in other words, sovereignty – and at the same time to maintain with Canada an economic association including a common currency; no change in political status resulting from these negotiations will be effected without approval by the people through another referendum; on these terms, do you give the Government of Quebec the mandate to negotiate the proposed agreement between Quebec and Canada?"

Yes

No

The date of the referendum was set for May 20, 1980; voters had thirty days to make up their minds. For inveterate gambler René Lévesque, it was like placing a bet. The wheel was turning. *Les jeux sont faits… rien ne va plus…* how would the game end?

∞

"When I left the meeting, last night, there had been no mention of a second referendum."

Jacques Parizeau was furious. At the end of his leader's speech he purportedly stormed out of the National Assembly's Blue Room. René Lévesque tried to hold his Minister of Finance back. Parizeau, who described himself as a real trooper, would not resign. Besides, like his leader, he thought that the majority of Quebecers would accept the government's proposal. In March 1980, parliamentary debates were in high gear, and the referendum campaign on track. Lévesque confided to the Péquistes: "The real work consists in persuading the undecided, *the federalists you can talk to.*" But he kept close watch on what was happening at the federal level. On February 18, the inevitable occurred: Pierre Trudeau was re-elected prime minister of Canada.

"And he's returning to the House of Commons with seventy-four out of seventy-five seats in Quebec!"

The leader of the sovereigntist forces was concerned. Contrary to what he had predicted, Claude Ryan, provincial Liberal leader since 1978, was no longer the sole advocate of a "no" vote; Lévesque now had to confront an opponent who was more clever and better-liked, Pierre Trudeau. Little by little the hope of a dazzling victory was receding. "We'll get it by the skin of our teeth," the most optimistic assumed. In fact, after the Referendum Bill was introduced in the National Assembly, it looked like the campaign would be difficult out in the field. Lévesque did not allow himself to get discouraged. Twenty years in political life had taught him to roll up his sleeves when need be. With his singular gift for stirring up enthusiasm in the darkest of times, he bounced back when anyone else would have been crushed.

As the time drew nearer, it seemed more and more inevitable that the referendum would fail. Lévesque fumed. He blamed the federal government, particularly Pierre Trudeau, who was promising to renew the constitution, and his ministers, who came up with all sorts of threats. But he kept fighting. "I just hope that a majority of francophones will show they support sovereignty."

But it was not to be. René Lévesque, who had tried for more than a month to convince Quebecers to vote "yes," had practically no voice left when five thousand supporters greeted him at the Paul Sauvé Centre in Montreal.

"I believe you have just said, 'Till the next time.'"

They had to accept the results: 59.6 per cent of voters had chosen "no," against 40.4 per cent who had voted "yes." Lévesque had toiled for thirteen years, only to be faced with this failure. However, on that day, he persuaded himself he would stick around for the next bout.

9

"... an old tree forgotten in the plains"

"It's all because of the Yvettes!"
The same refrain inevitably arose to explain the defeat and place blame.

"No, that's too easy."

René Lévesque was not among those using this scapegoat, even if he believed that Lise Payette, Minister responsible for the Status of Women, had blundered by comparing Claude Ryan's wife to an Yvette, the archetype of the docile, submissive little girl of school readers. Actually, the gaffe would have gone unnoticed if not for Lise Bissonnette's editorial in *Le Devoir*, which riled people up. In less than a few

Pierre Elliott Trudeau, prime minister of Canada, and Claude
Ryan, Quebec Liberal leader of the Opposition, in Quebec City,
before the referendum speech, May 14, 1980.

weeks, the "no's," in a burst of spontaneous solidarity, organized a huge rally. At the Montreal Forum on April 7, thousands of women, all Yvettes and proud of it, donned their "no" pins and waved banners featuring the federalist campaign slogan: *Plus j'y pense, plus c'est non* (The more I think about it, the more it's no). The rally was an incomparable media success. The Yvettes had hurt the sovereigntist campaign.

"At the time, I began to think we would lose," Lévesque maintained. "But I was puzzled. After all, Lise Payette had apologized in the House; I had told her myself she couldn't get around it."

A month before the PQ minister poked fun at the Liberal leader's wife, the polls had shown that the "yes" vote was losing ground. But politics is an unforgiving world. One blunder and a career is forever tarnished. Recalling the events of May 20, 1980, Lévesque confided: "That day, on the stage of the Paul Sauvé Centre, Madame Payette looked as if she were doing penance."

With one battle over, another began. As the referendum had taken place at the end of the first PQ government mandate, Lévesque began another election campaign. "We're going to win," he claimed. How could he be so sure? In the series of constitutional meetings planned by Trudeau, the Parti Québécois appeared to be the only negotiator able to represent the province's interests. On Monday, April 13, 1981, the Parti Québécois was easily re-elected with eighty members versus forty-two Liberals members.

"We are no accident of history," stressed René Lévesque, now heading the government in a second mandate.

After the speeches and interviews, Lévesque cele-
brated with his close collaborators. At one point in the
evening, the Télé-Métropole computer, gone mad,
announced the Union Nationale's spectacular recovery.
"For a moment, poor Roch Lasalle believed he was
premier of Quebec!" Laughter was in the air. This Parti
Québécois victory was a balm after the defeat of the
referendum, but it could not cure the gangrene eating
away at the party.

∞

René Lévesque approved Claude Morin's plan: "We
are going to forego our right to veto any constitutional
change; in exchange, we'll ask for the right to opt out
with financial compensation." To oppose unilateral
patriation of the Constitution, as proposed by Pierre
Trudeau, Quebec would form a united front with the
seven anglophone provinces who refused this power
grab. The group was nicknamed "the Gang of Eight."

On November 1, 1981, the Quebec delegation set
up in Hull, across the Ottawa River. René Lévesque
was confident enough to play poker in his free time.
Sent for at the last minute, Jacques Parizeau was scan-
dalized by the casual attitude prevailing in the Parti
Québécois leader's room: René Lévesque and his big-
wigs were surrounded by three women that the
Minister of Finance ironically dubbed the three
"muses." Disgusted, Parizeau rushed out of the meeting and returned to Quebec City. This scene did not
bode well.

∞

When Quebecers voted "no," Pierre Trudeau decided it was time to act. Eighteen months following this victory, the Canadian prime minister convened the ten provincial premiers at the Ottawa Congress Centre. Patriating the Canadian Constitution was an obsession with Trudeau. In politics since 1965, he wanted this to be his political legacy. He intended to give Canada back its entire Constitution, which until then had been a British law modifiable only upon request to the Parliament of Westminster. This first step allowed him to include in the Canadian Constitution the Charter of Rights and Freedoms he so prized.

Pierre Trudeau would not allow Quebec to steal his dream.

Would this 1981 federal-provincial conference end in rancour and recrimination as usual? On the morning of November 4, Lévesque dropped a bombshell. He intimated that he was be ready to meet Trudeau's challenge of holding a referendum at the national level, two years after the patriation of the Constitution. "You," the Canadian prime minister had said to René Lévesque, "you, the great democrat – don't tell me you're afraid of a fight?" Out of bravado, Lévesque had given in.

A poor strategy? Did Lévesque want to break the pact he had concluded earlier with the other seven allied provinces? In the afternoon, Lévesque seemed to change his mind: "The proposal of a national referendum is full of red tape," he informed journalists. "Trudeau has added to it a host of unacceptable conditions."

On the evening of November 4, when the Quebec delegation withdrew to l'Auberge de la Chaudière, Lévesque shook hands with his colleagues. The night would be short, the awakening rude.

∞

"They stabbed us in the back!"

René Lévesque was talking to Corinne on the phone.

"While we were sleeping, the premiers of the other provinces met in the kitchen of the Congress Centre to hatch a plan. With us out of the picture, they reached an agreement that Trudeau accepted... They pulled a fast one!... Someone said it resembled the Night of the Long Knives. Quebec has lost everything: the right to veto as well as the right to opt out with compensation. Now we're all alone."

Was he crying? His companion sensed he was devastated. At one point he spoke of getting on a plane for Quebec City. That would be a mistake. Once again he had to explain failure, assume responsibility, and live with the consequences.

On November 5, thousands of supporters greeted a broken man at Quebec City's Ancienne-Lorette Airport. Days passed. Lévesque was no longer the same. Within his party, dissension increased.

Winning the April 1981 election, despite initial appearances, had proved ruinous. The climate of solidarity that had followed 1976 was sorely lacking in the second PQ mandate. Lévesque, distant, gruff, and aggressive, no longer tolerated his ministers' demands, and found caucus meetings unbearable. Discussions often turned sour. The leader had difficulty containing temper tantrums and personality conflicts.

Lévesque's private life was also disorganized. His opponents took note of his escapades; the slightest breach of conduct could be used against him. Still inclined to seduce women, he tried to cheat the passing of time, making easy conquests as a means of reassurance.

But while he drowned himself in this whirl of activity, reality caught up with him. In December, the National Convention turned out to be a tough test of strength. He had to explain the failure of the last federal-provincial conference to supporters who were growing impatient with the party's slowness in achieving Quebec sovereignty. Lévesque was disillusioned. Being in power had left him exhausted. To defend himself, he became furious. The newspapers reported his gutter language, unbefitting his position. He spoke incessantly of "soiled sheets," of "dirty diapers." He was swearing right and left noted an editorial writer who deplored his "filthy language." Several people no longer recognized this embittered man who earlier had been known for his sense of humour in the face of adversity. Truth be told, Lévesque was shattered: the defeat of November 1981 added to the failure of the referendum. He saw himself as a loser and had lost the strength to fight.

At the Montreal convention, he did not intend to push the constitutional project any further. From now on, he wanted to speak of economics. Recently, the Minister of Finance had showed him the figures of the deficit, which were catastrophic. This time it was as head of government that he faced his supporters. But they did not share his concerns.

"I suggest that we forget about the project of association with Canada," one convention delegate maintained.

Another went further: they had to take away the rights of anglophones. The next election would have to be a referendum and be validated by the number of seats alone, not by the total vote. When he heard people applaud the resolution demanding FLQ prisoners be transferred to a Quebec prison, René Lévesque was shocked. At the closing of the convention, his speech to the delegates was pitiless, his criticism sharp. Admitting he felt at odds, he added:

"Instinctively I thought of resigning as president of the Parti Québécois. But I told myself: Too many people would be pleased. So I thought about it. And I'm staying."

René Lévesque was nobody's fool. He was directly alluding to the people in his party who wanted him to leave. How much longer could he suppress their wishes?

∞

The *renérendum*: a somewhat wry play on words.

"It wasn't my idea," admitted Lévesque, "but it seemed to me interesting to hold a referendum among party members. We were right: almost everyone was on my side. It was time to get back to work – immediately."

This storm had barely blown over when another, stronger and more threatening, arose. If expenses continued to rise, Quebec would be bankrupt: there was a seven-hundred-thousand-dollar deficit! Imposing a freeze or cancelling public servants' salary increases was out of the question. "I'll never go back on my word!" responded Minister of Finance Jacques Parizeau.

After days of discussions, which, confided Lévesque "were enough to drive a person crazy," he ended up approving Parizeau's solution, which consisted of paying the increases until the end of December and then recouping the amount of the deficit in three months. What analysts referred to as "the swimming pool" – emphasizing a resemblance between the slope of the wage curve they wanted to impose and a pool basin – brought the PQ government to pass extraordinary legislation imposing non-negotiated settlements. The three hundred thousand public servants were outraged and felt betrayed. René Lévesque became the scapegoat of this economic strategy; disgusted, the unions burned him in effigy. Later, in an interview, he admitted:

"What hurt me the most, was seeing a sign that read *Lévesque, the butcher of New Carlisle*. It awakened painful childhood memories, the social injustice in the Gaspé. I felt I was being personally attacked."

The government's intransigence had damaging repercussions on the Parti Québécois. Its demise was swift. From three hundred thousand members at the beginning of 1982, membership dwindled to a mere seventy-eight thousand by mid-1983. More than ever,

Lévesque had the impression he'd failed in his dream, was alone in his trek across the desert. A Shakespearian hero: Hamlet in doubt, King Lear stripped of everything, Richard III without his kingdom.

∞

A little gin, a few drops of vermouth, a twist of lemon: the martini was on the table, next to an open pack of cigarettes. Late November. That evening, René Lévesque holed up in his house on rue d'Auteuil in Quebec City. If only he could wipe out 1984, when one misfortune followed another! People said he drank too much. Some even suggested asking the lieutenant-governor to dismiss him from his duties, a kind of impeachment.

Lévesque vacillated – a word that crops up often in his diary. Since January, he had gone back to a habit he'd had as a teenager: he wrote to organize his thoughts, to avoid making the same mistakes. He suffered a great deal. Claude Charron's resignation in late 1982 – after being accused of shoplifting at Eaton's – was a blow. Against his will, he'd agreed that "the nut," as he'd fondly nicknamed him, leave. On the other hand, Claude Morin's departure, three years earlier, had given rise to more ambivalent feelings. Lorraine Lagacé, a public servant at the Department of Intergovernmental Affairs, had asked for a meeting in the Montreal office.

"Monsieur Lévesque, your minister Claude Morin is spying for the Royal Canadian Mounted Police! They're paying him: four hundred dollars per meeting."

Shocked, he'd paled visibly. Could it be? After seeking information from colleagues who were better informed, the PQ leader felt he had been betrayed. While Morin swore he had never given any information that could endanger Quebec, Lévesque became aware of how vulnerable he was. He was being openly deceived, and hadn't a clue, blindly trusting those around him. A serious error in judgment on the part of head of state.

Misfortune dogged him. Robert Bourassa returned as Liberal leader. The economist had gained status in European universities, and now 66 per cent of voters returned his Liberal Party to power. Then came the latest poll, making headlines: "One in two Quebecers believes that René Lévesque must go even if he is carrying out his responsibilities well." Not surprisingly, the ninth Parti Québécois convention ended in failure!

Lévesque took another cigarette. Smoking was his passion, a need that possessed him, as if wanting to reduce all his worries to ashes.

He told himself that he could have resorted to irrational politics in April 1982, when Pierre Trudeau was celebrating the patriation of the Canadian Constitution with great pomp, rejoicing and looking on triumphantly as Queen Elizabeth II signed the official documents. He could have persisted in wanting sovereignty at any cost. "But I took a risk."

⚭

Lévesque was dredging up terribly painful images that gnawed away at him. At the National Convention of the Parti Québécois in June 1984 everything started to collapse. Contrary to his expectations, the most radical delegates managed to have a resolution passed that the next election would be a referendum.

Lévesque had to find a solution. He couldn't let the extremists have their way or the PQ would head straight to the slaughterhouse.

Strategists surrounding the PQ leader sought a way out. Why not accept the offer of Brian Mulroney, the new leader of the federal Conservative Party? A few weeks later, on September 4, Mulroney would defeat the Liberals. One of his first promises consisted of including Quebec in Canadian Confederation. "Honourably and enthusiastically," emphasized Lucien Bouchard, who would become a minister in the Mulroney government.

They called it "le beau risque."

A last chance. Put sovereignty on the back burner and try to strike up an alliance with the least arrogant of the federalists. It was a kind of third option, one that involved asking Ottawa for more power. Yes, it was settled. René Lévesque extended his hand to the Conservatives and headed out in a new direction. He had better watch his step!

But things turned sour: between July and November 1984, everything went downhill.

"I played my hand badly," René Lévesque acknowledged later. "When I was in Fort Prével, in the Gaspé, I told everyone that we needed a moratorium on the constitutional issue. Stop talking about it for a while. But why did I let Pierre Marc Johnson give *Le Devoir* an interview?"

Lévesque drained his martini in one gulp and lit another cigarette. He took a hard look at things, trying to understand why he had ended up so alone. The simple words of a poem by Pamphile Le May haunted him: "je suis comme le vieil arbre dans la plaine" / I'm like the old tree forgotten in the plains.

In mid-November, Lévesque stated that he was putting the idea of sovereignty-association on the back burner. Mentioning the "need for sovereignty," twelve ministers made a public declaration that resembled a coup attempt. The leader answered them with a letter in which his words stoked the hostility that had been dormant since the successive failures of the referendum and the Night of the Long Knives in 1981. From then on, as far as he was concerned, there would never be a referendum election. He added, "anyway, what form would this Nation-State take? We've pictured it since the sixties, believed it was so close at hand, so vital. I don't know any more about it than anyone else."

Believed. The use of the past tense shocked the hard-liners.

The war was on. There would be losers on all sides.

○○

On rue d'Auteuil, René Lévesque spread out in front of him letters from those who'd resigned.

"A minister can't just resign!" he had exclaimed in jest. But he was wrong. By the end of November, twelve ministers had left. Old war buddies, some of whom he had known since 1970, for almost fifteen years. Most of all he regretted the departure of

Dr. Camille Laurin, whom he respected and sometimes, feared. "A shrink – always rummaging around in
the unconscious!"

The next day, at the National Assembly, Lévesque
no longer sat next to his twelve former ministers.
Would he avoid looking at them? Greet his friends? It
was an ordeal. Still wanting to believe he could wash
his dirty linen in public, Lévesque contemplated calling a special convention before the end of January. The
prodigal sons, he thought, would return to their father.
And he was ready to forgive them.

∞

"Where is he?"

Corinne, on vacation in Barbados, hadn't been
able to stop her husband. Without warning, one morning, he had boarded a plane to Montreal. On the other
end of the line, Yves Michaud reassured her: René was
at his office in the Hydro Québec building.

"He's tired. Burnt out. We're going to try and convince him to go to the hospital for tests."

News spread quickly among the journalists cooling
their heels in the corridors of Quebec City's Enfant-
Jésus Hospital. "Is it true that the premier has a brain
tumour?" No. It was lung cancer. He smoked too
much. In the end, the gossipmongers were silenced,
proved wrong across the board. After several tests,
Lévesque's physician was highly encouraging: at his
age, however, he had to slow down and watch his diet.
"Let's speed things up, so I can get back to work," said
Lévesque. Mostly he had in mind the January conven-

tion, his last chance. Bolstered by his doctor's advice, he felt ready to overcome this new hurdle.

But had he correctly gauged his chances of success?

In 1967, it was he who had left the Liberal Party. This time, it was his own PQ staff members who were leaving. Right to the end, they clashed with their leader, who no longer wanted to hear tell of a referendum election. At the Palais des congrès, a third of the delegates left the room shouting: "Le Québec aux Québécois!" "Quebec for Quebecers!" Six hundred people out of two thousand were led by Dr. Laurin, prestigiously dubbed the "Father of Bill 101." Decidedly, fortune was no longer smiling on René Lévesque. The convention in early 1985 confirmed once and for all that the orthodox members and the revisionists were irreconcilable.

In the middle of the disputes, Lévesque was a shadow of his former self.

But he didn't give up; he announced he would lead the PQ in the next election, slated to take place before the end of the year. He claimed he'd never seen his troops in such good shape – was he exaggerating? The financing campaign was going well, and the leader of the PQ was ready to throw himself into the ring.

∞

On June 25, 1985, the National Assembly was celebrating. Twenty-five years earlier, as a Liberal member in the Montreal-Laurier riding, Lévesque had entered political life. Now, following the ceremonial speeches, Lévesque greeted his loyal friend, Marc-André Bédard. It was almost seven o'clock when he withdrew into his office. At the end of the evening, after the national news broadcast, the vice-president of the Parti Québécois received a letter. She recognized the handwriting. It began: "Dear Nadia."

The statement was brief, laconic, cold, in the image of a man who detested effusiveness and sentimentality: René Lévesque was resigning as president of the Parti Québécois; he would, however, act as interim president until the fall, until his successor, Pierre Marc Johnson, arrived.

Only a few close friends had been informed of the decision he had made two months earlier. That evening, he felt free.

∞

October 1986: René Lévesque published his memoirs under the ironic title *Attendez que je me rappelle* ("Wait Till I Remember"). One hundred thousand copies were sold. The English translation was published under the title *Memoirs*. After taking time out to travel in August 1987, Lévesque accepted a spot on a news show, *Point de vue sur l'actualité* on CKAC, a Montreal radio station. During the Semaine de la Francophonie, he was also featured in special broadcasts on Télé-Métropole. Happy to return to journalism, his first love, Lévesque was particularly interested in what then was the hot topic, free trade with the U.S. He barely spoke of sovereignty anymore, a task he left to Jacques Parizeau, new leader of the Parti Québécois.

On Friday, October 30, the day before Halloween, he joked on the radio with Jacques Proulx. He was spirited, charming. Leaving the station on Peel Street, he called to everyone:

"Bye for now!"

But he would not return. He had less than two days left to live.

∞

RENÉ LÉVESQUE IS DEAD. These four words made newspaper headlines on Monday, November 2, 1987. The day before, in his apartment on Nun's Island, the former premier had experienced chest pains. Transported to hospital, he died from the effects of a heart attack. He was sixty-five.

The praise, from all political parties, was unanimous. Even though Lévesque was no longer premier of Quebec, Robert Bourassa's Liberal government granted him the funeral of a head of state. In Montreal, thousands of people waited for hours to file past his remains. Their mourning was genuine, their homages spontaneous: "it's as if we've lost a friend," vowed strangers who had never approached him. René Lévesque was part of the Quebec family. The man was in the image of Quebec, with its doubts and contradictions. "The Poet-Leader," Jacques Parizeau nicknamed him.

At the Saint-Michel de Sillery cemetery, on René Lévesque's tombstone, Félix Leclerc's words summed up the pride the leader had inspired: "The first page of Quebec's true history has just ended. Henceforth his name will join the select few who can be called liberators of the people."

Claude Morin, Pierre Elliott Trudeau, René Lévesque (back), and Jean Chrétien in 1981, during the Constitutional Conference in Ottawa.

Chronology of
René Lévesque
(1922-1987)

Compliled by Michèle Vanasse

RENÉ LÉVESQUE AND QUEBEC	CANADA AND THE WORLD
1920 Louis-Alexandre Taschereau, a Liberal, becomes premier of Quebec.	**1920** Robert Borden resigns and Arthur Meighen becomes the new prime minister of Canada. In the United States (U.S.), women receive the right to vote.
1921 The Canadian and Catholic Confederation of Labour (CCCL) is founded; it becomes the Confederation of National Trade Unions (CNTU) in 1960. The Public Charities Act is adopted and the Liquor Commission is created.	**1921** Mackenzie King, a Liberal, is elected prime minister of Canada. In China, Mao Zedong and others found the Chinese Communist Party.

RENÉ LÉVESQUE AND QUEBEC

1922
René Lévesque is born on August 24 at Cambellton Hospital in New Brunswick. He is the son of Diane Dionne and Dominique Lévesque, a lawyer in New Carlisle

In Montreal, the newspaper *La Presse* founds CKAC, Canada's first French-language radio station.

1927
René enters bilingual school Number 1 in New Carlisle.

The Taschereau government is re-elected.

1929
Montreal's mayor and Member of the Legislative Assembly Camillien Houde is chosen to succeed Arthur Sauvé as leader of the Conservative Party of Quebec.

1930
An act known as the *Loi de l'aide aux chômeurs* is passed to help the unemployed.

1932
The Jeunes-Canada movement is founded; André Laurendeau writes its manifesto.

CANADA AND THE WORLD

1922
In Italy, the march on Rome takes place and Benito Mussolini rises to power.

The Soviet convention founds the Union of Soviet Socialist Republics (U.S.S.R.) Joseph Stalin is elected General Secretary of the Bolshevik Party.

1927
The Judicial Committee of the Privy Council of London awards Labrador to Newfoundland.

In Vietnam, Ho Chi Minh founds the Vietnamese Communist Party.

1929
In the U.S., the New York Stock Exchange collapses on Thursday, October 24, marking the beginning of the Great Depression that will extend throughout the Western World.

1930
Richard Bennett's Conservatives are victorious in the Canadian federal election.

1932
In Canada, the Co-operative Commonwealth Federation (CCF) is founded; it becomes the New Democratic Party (NDP) in 1961.

RENÉ LÉVESQUE AND QUEBEC	CANADA AND THE WORLD

1933
René enters the Séminaire des Jésuites, founded in 1926 in Gaspé.

A group of Jesuits and lay people publish the *Programme de restauration sociale*.

Maurice Duplessis is elected leader of the Quebec Conservative Party.

1933
In the U.S., Franklin D. Roosevelt becomes president; Prohibition ends.

In Germany, Adolf Hitler becomes Chancellor.

1934
The Action libérale nationale is founded, led by Paul Gouin, son of Lomer Gouin and grandson of Honoré Mercier.

Adrien Arcand founds the Parti national social chrétien (Christian Nationalist Socialist Party), an extreme right-wing party in favour of establishing a fascist regime.

1934
Mao Zedong, leading the Chinese Communists, begins the Long March in order to obtain active support from the people and carry out a peasant revolution rather than a proletarian one.

1935
The Liberal Party wins the election, defeating Paul Gouin's Action libérale nationale and Maurice Duplessis' Conservative Party.

The Conservative Party and Paul Gouin's Action libérale nationale unite, which leads to Maurice Duplessis founding the Union Nationale.

1935
Mackenzie King, a Liberal, is re-elected prime minister of Canada.

In France, the first television broadcasts occur.

1936
Premier Louis-Alexandre Taschereau resigns and is replaced by Adélard Godbout.

1936
In Canada, the Canadian Broadcasting Corporation (CBC), known in French as Société Radio-Canada (SRC), is created.

RENÉ LÉVESQUE AND QUEBEC

Maurice Duplessis is elected leader of the Union Nationale.

Creation of the farm credit system in Quebec, known as the Crédit agricole provincial.

The Old Age Pension Act is passed in Quebec.

1937
Dominique Lévesque dies at age forty-eight.

Duplessis enacts the Padlock Act, which forbids any person to use his or her home to propagate communism. The Fair Wage Act and the Needy Mothers' Assistance Act are passed.

1938
René becomes an announcer on CHNC, a New Carlisle radio station, during the summer vacation.

Lévesque's mother Diane Dionne and her children move to Quebec City and René enters Collège Garnier.

1939
Diane Dionne marries Albert Pelletier, a lawyer and friend of the family.

Adélard Godbout's Liberal Party wins the election thanks to the

CANADA AND THE WORLD

In France, Léon Blum's Front populaire win the election; their party brings together leftist forces to fight Fascism.

Nazi Germany and Fascist Italy form an alliance.

In Spain, Civil War between General Franco's Nationalists and the Republicans begins.

1937
In Canada, the Rowell-Sirois Commission studies federal-provincial relations.

In Great Britain, George VI is crowned.

1938
The Anschluss occurs: in a show of force, Hitler annexes Austria to the German Reich.

The Munich Agreement is signed: France and England, fearing a conflict, agree to the annexation of the Sudeten, a part of Czechoslovakia, by Hitler.

1939
The Second World War begins: on September 1, Germany invades Poland, inciting France and Great Britain to declare war.

RENÉ LÉVESQUE AND QUEBEC

federal Minister of Justice Ernest Lapointe's promise that there will be no conscription.

1940
In February, while in "Philosophie 1," the second-last year of the *cours classique* in the *collège classique* system, René Lévesque is expelled from Collège Garnier and admitted to the Séminaire de Québec.

He works part-time as an announcer at CKCV radio station.

The Godbout government grants women the right to vote.

Msgr. Joseph Charbonneau is appointed Archbishop of Montreal.

1941
After obtaining his bachelor's degree in May, René Lévesque enrols in the Faculty of Law at Université Laval in September.

Albert Pelletier, Diane Dionne's second husband and René's stepfather, dies.

1942
René Lévesque's play, *Princesse à marier*, starring Lucien Côté, opens at the Palais Montcalm. It flops.

CANADA AND THE WORLD

On September 10, Canada declares war on Germany.

The U.S. remains neutral.

In Spain, General Franco is victorious.

1940
In Great Britain, Winston Churchill becomes prime minister.

Italy enters the war alongside Germany.

France falls: while Maréchal Pétain's government sets up in Vichy, Général Charles de Gaulle urges the French to resist and forms the Free French Forces.

1941
In Canada, CBC and Radio-Canada launch their News Service.

The U.S.S.R. enters the war against Germany.

In the U.S., the Japanese attack Pearl Harbor, Hawaii on December 7. The Americans declare war on Japan and on its allies, Germany and Italy.

1942
Following a plebiscite held April 27, the Canadian Parliament passes Bill 80 in favour of conscription.

RENÉ LÉVESQUE AND QUEBEC	CANADA AND THE WORLD

Lévesque is hired as an announcer at CBV-Quebec, a Radio-Canada affiliate.

Maxime Raymond founds the Bloc populaire, a federal party of Quebecers opposed to conscription.

The Legislative Assembly declares it is against conscription.

In France, almost half the Canadians who participate in Allied troop landings in Dieppe are killed.

1943
Legislation on compulsory education in Quebec is adopted.

1943
In Canada, Churchill and Roosevelt meet at the Quebec Conference, held in order to accelerate planning the Allies' landing on the Italian peninsula and in Normandy.

The State establishes a commission to prepare a universal health insurance plan; the following year Duplessis will dissolve the commission.

1944
René Lévesque abandons his legal studies and enters the Office of War Information. He leaves for London where he works for the *Voice of America*.

1944
In Italy, Americans march on Rome.

In France, on June 6, the Allies land in Normandy under the command of American General Dwight Eisenhower.

The Godbout government brings the electricity company Montreal Light, Heat and Power into public ownership and enacts the law establishing Hydro-Québec.

In the Pacific, there is a massive intervention by American troops, who drive back the Japanese and advance to Japan.

Maurice Duplessis is returned to office.

1945
René Lévesque, liaison officer and war correspondent, is assigned to General Patton's division in France. He sees the ravages of war in Alsace, Austria, Italy, and Germany; he enters the Dachau

1945
In Canada, Mackenzie King is re-elected.

In Europe, Germany surrenders on May 7, ending the war. The Nazi death camps are discovered.

RENÉ LÉVESQUE AND QUEBEC

death camp with the American army.

Upon his return to Canada, René Lévesque is hired by *La voix du Canada*, Radio-Canada's international service. He settles in Montreal.

The provincial government asks the federal government for the right to tax individuals and corporations, as well as estates and gasoline.

A rural electrification network in Quebec and the Department of Natural Resources are created.

1946
Àt Radio-Canada, Lévesque introduces *Les actualités canadiennes*. He meets journalist Judith Jasmin.

The Department of Social Welfare and Youth is created.

1947
René Lévesque marries Louise, daughter of Eugène L'Heureux, eminent journalist and ex-editor in chief of *L'Action catholique*.

Hydro-Québec takes possession of Montreal Light, Heat and Power.

CANADA AND THE WORLD

In Japan, an atomic bomb is dropped on Hiroshima on August 6 and on Nagasaki August 9; Japan surrenders September 2.

The First Assembly of the United Nations (UN) is held; its role is to maintain peace in the world and ensure that fundamental human rights are upheld.

In the U.S., President Roosevelt dies and is succeeded by Harry Truman.

1946
Winston Churchill names the countries under Soviet domination "the iron curtain countries."

The Indochina (Vietnam) conflict begins.

In the U.S., the first electronic computer is developed.

1947
Canada becomes a member of the UN.

India is granted its independence by Great Britain.

In the U.S., the "Truman Doctrine" seeks to check the progress of Communism, and the Marshall

RENÉ LÉVESQUE AND QUEBEC	CANADA AND THE WORLD
	Plan aims at the reconstruction of Europe.
1948 Pierre, the Lévesques' first child, is born.	**1948** Liberal Louis Saint-Laurent becomes prime minister of Canada.
Maurice Duplessis's Union Nationale is re-elected. The Fleur-de-lis flag is adopted.	In India, nationalist leader Gandhi is assassinated.
Refus global, the manifesto of the Automatistes, led by Paul-Émile Borduas, appears.	David Ben-Gurion proclaims the state of Israel.
1949 Lévesque hosts his own program, *Les interviews de René Lévesque*, on shortwave radio and *Journalistes au micro* on the national network.	**1949** In Canada, Louis Saint-Laurent's Liberals are victorious in the federal election. The country becomes a member of the North American Treaty Organization (NATO). Newfoundland becomes Canada's tenth province.
Asbestos workers strike in Asbestos, Quebec; workers' demonstrations are harshly quelled, but many members of the clergy, including the Archbishop of Montreal, Msgr. Charbonneau, are sympathetic to the strikers. Hydro-Québec acquires property, factories, and dams on the Ottawa River.	The Federal Republic of Germany (FRG), part of the western bloc, and the German Democratic Republic (GDR), part of the Soviet bloc, are formed.
	In China, Mao Zedong proclaims the People's Republic of China.
	In South Africa, apartheid is implemented.
1950 Claude, the Lévesques' second child, is born.	**1950** The Korean War begins when Communist North Korea invades South Korea. UN troops intervene

RENÉ LÉVESQUE AND QUEBEC

Gérard Pelletier and Pierre Elliott Trudeau found *Cité libre*, a magazine attacking traditional nationalistic themes.

Msgr. Joseph Charbonneau, Archbishop of Montreal, resigns.

1951
René Lévesque goes to South Korea as a reporter for Radio-Canada's *La revue de l'actualité* and *Le Petit Journal*, and also spends time in Japan. In Canada, Lévesque covers the royal visit of Princess Elizabeth and Prince Philip for Radio-Canada.

He becomes a film reviewer on the program *La revue des arts et lettres*.

The first Youth Protection Act is passed.

1952
The Union Nationale and Maurice Duplessis are re-elected but with a reduced majority against Georges-Émile Lapalme's Liberals.

The Department of Transport is created.

1953
René Lévesque leaves the international service and is placed in charge of radio programming for

CANADA AND THE WORLD

under the command of American General Douglas MacArthur.

1951
Princess Elizabeth makes her first royal visit to Canada with her husband Philip, Duke of Edinburgh.

The Massey Commission on Arts, Letters, and Sciences publishes its report, advocating federal government support of the arts in Canada.

In Germany, Allied occupation ends.

1952
Canadian French-language television begins with station CBFT.

In the U.S., Dwight D. Eisenhower, a Republican, is elected president.

In Great Britain, Elizabeth II becomes Queen of the Commonwealth upon the death of her father, King George VI.

1953
Coronation of Queen Elizabeth June 2, 1953.

RENÉ LÉVESQUE AND QUEBEC	CANADA AND THE WORLD

Radio-Canada. With Judith Jasmin, he creates and hosts the program *Carrefour*.

Duplessis refuses federal subsidies for institutions of higher learning.

The Tremblay Commission, a royal commission of inquiry on constitutional problems, is created.

In the U.S.S.R., Nikita Khrushchev becomes General Secretary of the Communist Party upon the death of Stalin.

The Korean war ends.

1954
A provincial income tax on personal income is introduced; the federal government is obliged to reduce its own taxation by 10 per cent.

1954
The Indochina Conflict ends. The Geneva Accord divides Vietnam into two states: North Vietnam and South Vietnam. The Algerian War begins.

1955
Reporter René Lévesque travels to the U.S.S.R. with Minister of Foreign Affairs Lester B. Pearson, his advisors, and just one other journalist.

Carrefour, a daily radio broadcast, becomes a television program. Lévesque also takes part in the program *Conférence de presse*.

1955
The Warsaw Pact sets up a military alliance between the East Bloc countries.

In South Vietnam, the Republic is proclaimed; Ngo Dinh Diem is president.

1956
Suzanne, the Lévesques' daughter, is born.

Now a freelancer, René Lévesque hosts *Les aventures de Max Fuchs*, a program for young people. He is given the weekly public affairs program, *Point de mire*.

1956
In Hungary, insurrection occurs in Budapest. Soviet troops intervene.

In the Middle East, nationalization of the Suez Canal is announced, provoking Israel to attack Egypt. French and British troops land in Suez to protect the canal. The UN intervenes, as does Canadian diplomat Lester B. Pearson.

RENÉ LÉVESQUE AND QUEBEC	CANADA AND THE WORLD
Maurice Duplessis and the Union Nationale are re-elected.	
1957	**1957**
The Quebec Federation of Labour (QFL) is created.	Conservative John Diefenbaker is elected prime minister of Canada. Lester B. Pearson receives the Nobel Peace Prize.
Raymond Barbeau founds the Alliance laurentienne, a movement advocating Quebec independence.	In Europe, the European Economic Community (EEC) is created.
	In the U.S.S.R., Sputnik, the first artificial satellite, is launched.
1958	**1958**
Lévesque returns to radio and becomes the morning host of *Au lendemain de la veille*.	In Canada, the hospitalization insurance program is implemented; provinces share the costs.
Réal Caouette creates a new party, le Ralliement des créditistes.	In France, Charles de Gaulle becomes president.
1959	**1959**
Premier Maurice Duplessis dies in office and is succeeded by Paul Sauvé.	In Canada, the St. Lawrence Seaway is officially opened by Queen Elizabeth II.
Radio-Canada producers strike and René Lévesque becomes actively involved. Afterwards, *Point de mire* is cancelled; Lévesque takes part in *Premier plan*.	In Cuba, Fidel Castro's Socialist Revolution takes place.
1960	**1960**
After Paul Sauvé dies and Antonio Barrette is defeated, Jean Lesage's Liberal Party rises to power, an event which marks the beginning of the Quiet Revolution.	Democrat John F. Kennedy is elected president of the United States.

RENÉ LÉVESQUE AND QUEBEC	CANADA AND THE WORLD
René Lévesque is elected Liberal member for Montreal-Laurier. He is named Minister of Hydro-electric Resources and Public Works.	
Marcel Chaput and André D'Allemagne found the Rassemblement pour l'indépendance nationale (RIN).	

1961

René Lévesque is named Minister of Natural Resources, a department that merges Water Resources and Mines.

The Department of Cultural Affairs, the Office de la langue française and the Conseil des Arts du Québec are created.

The Parent Commission is set up; its goal is to examine how education is organized and financed.

1961

The New Democratic Party of Canada (NDP) is founded, and Tommy Douglas is elected leader.

The United States enters the Vietnam War by sending in military advisors.

In East Germany, the Berlin Wall is built.

Soviet astronaut Yuri Gagarin becomes the first man to fly in space.

1962

The struggle for nationalizing electricity unfolds at the election, which is won by the Liberal Party, whose slogan is *Maîtres chez nous* (Masters in our own house). René Lévesque is re-elected.

The Société générale de financement, or SGF (General Investment Corporation) is created.

1962

Following a naval blockade by the U.S., the U.S.S.R. withdraws its missiles from Cuba. The peaceful solution to the Cuban Missile Crisis emphasizes the détente between East and West.

RENÉ LÉVESQUE AND QUEBEC

1963
Hydro-Québec takes over large private electricity companies.

The RIN becomes a political party.

Members of the Front de libération du Québec (FLQ) hold violent demonstrations and plant their first bombs.

1964
Following the first recommendations by the Parent Commission, a Department of Education is created. Legislation is passed to create the Labour Code as well as the Rental Board.

Pierre Bourgault becomes president of the RIN.

Another sovereigntist party, the Ralliement national, is founded.

Samedi de la matraque ("Truncheon Saturday"): brutal repression in Quebec City during the visit of Queen Elizabeth II.

1965
René Lévesque is named Minister of the newly created department, Family and Social Services.

Legislation is passed to create the Civil Service Act, the Société québécoise d'exploration minière, or SOQUEM (Quebec Mining Exploration Company) and the

CANADA AND THE WORLD

1963
Liberal Lester B. Pearson becomes prime minister of Canada.

In the United States, President John F. Kennedy is assassinated in Dallas, Texas.

1964
In the U.S., under Kennedy's successor Lyndon B. Johnson, the escalation of the war in Vietnam continues and racial rioting at home increases.

In the U.S.S.R., Khrushchev is dismissed from his duties and replaced by Leonid Brezhnev and Alexei Kosygin.

1965
Canada adopts the Maple Leaf flag. Preliminary report of the Laurendeau-Dunton Commission on Bilingualism and Biculturalism.

In the U.S., Martin Luther King leads a march for the rights of black Americans in Alabama.

RENÉ LÉVESQUE AND QUEBEC	CANADA AND THE WORLD
Caisse de dépôt et placement du Québec (Quebec Deposit and Investment Fund).	
A violent demonstration occurs in Montreal on Victoria Day.	
1966 René Lévesque is re-elected as Liberal member for Montreal-Laurier, but the Liberal Party loses the election. Daniel Johnson, leader of the Union Nationale, becomes premier.	**1966** In the U.S.S.R., Leonid Brezhnev becomes General Secretary of the Communist Party. In China, Mao launches the People's Cultural Revolution.
Lévesque writes a weekly column in the newspaper *Dimanche-Matin*.	
Pierre Vallières publishes *Nègres blancs d'Amérique* (translated as *White Niggers of America*).	
1967 René Lévesque resigns from the Liberal Party and sits as an independent. He founds the Mouvement souveraineté-association (Sovereignty-Association Movement).	**1967** Following recommendations from the Laurendeau-Dunton Commission, the federal government decides to promote bilingualism within the public service of Canada.
The first CEGEPs are created and power stations Manic 1 and 2 are commissioned.	In Greece, the Regime of the Colonels begins.
Expo takes place in Montreal. During his visit, French President Charles de Gaulle proclaims his famous "Vive le Québec libre!"	A new Israeli-Arab conflict, the Six Day War, erupts in the Middle East.

RENÉ LÉVESQUE AND QUEBEC

1968
René Lévesque launches his book *Option Québec* in January and in October founds the Parti Québécois from the Mouvement souveraineté-association and from sovereigntist forces consolidated within the Ralliement national and the RIN. He is party president.

Several bombs exploded in Montreal, notably at Eaton's department store and on the floor of the stock exchange.

Daniel Johnson dies; Jean-Jacques Bertrand succeeds him.

Radio-Québec is founded and the Université du Québec created.

1969
Economist Jacques Parizeau joins the Parti Québécois.

Despite numerous protests, legislation is passed for Bill 63, giving parents free choice of the language of instruction for their children.

Two departments are created: Public Service and Communications, as well as Loto-Québec.

1970
October Crisis: British diplomat James Richard Cross and Minister of Labour Pierre Laporte are kidnapped by the Front de libération du Québec (FLQ); Pierre Laporte is murdered.

CANADA AND THE WORLD

1968
Liberal Pierre Elliott Trudeau is elected prime minister of Canada.

In the U.S., Martin Luther King, advocate of non-violence, and Robert Kennedy, a defender of minority rights, are assassinated.

Republican Richard Nixon is elected president.

In May 1968, student protests occur worldwide.

In Czechoslovakia, Warsaw Pact troops invade Prague, ending Czech hopes of liberation from the Soviet yoke.

1969
American astronaut Neil Armstrong is the first man to walk on the moon.

Yasser Arafat becomes president of the Palestine Liberation Organization (PLO).

1970
Following the kidnapping of James Richard Cross and Pierre Laporte, the government of Canada invokes the War Measures Act, suspending certain civil liberties.

RENÉ LÉVESQUE AND QUEBEC

Medicare, a universal health insurance plan, is implemented.

The Liberal Party led by Robert Bourassa is victorious in the provincial election. Lévesque is defeated in Montreal-Laurier but seven PQ members are elected. Lévesque becomes a columnist at the *Journal de Montreal* and the *Journal de Québec*.

1971

The Department of Social Affairs is created and CLSCs (local community service centres) are established.

1972

Government employees go on strike and form a common front; union leaders who defy the Bourassa government are imprisoned.

1973

The RCMP steals the list of Parti Québécois members in Montreal. Robert Bourassa's Liberal Party wins the provincial election; the Parti Québécois elects six members, but René Lévesque is defeated in his Dorion riding.

The report of the Gendron Commission on the situation of the French language and linguistic rights is submitted.

CANADA AND THE WORLD

Former French president Charles de Gaulle dies.

In Chile, Salvador Allende is elected president.

1971

In Canada, the Victoria Conference fails. Quebec refuses the federal government's proposal to patriate and amend the Constitution.

1972

Pierre Elliott Trudeau and the Liberal Party are re-elected in the Canadian federal election.

Richard Nixon is the first U.S. president to visit Communist China.

1973

In the U.S., the White House is involved in the Watergate affair.

North Vietnam and the United States sign a ceasefire agreement in Paris.

In the Middle East, the Israeli-Arab conflict (the Yom Kippur War) leads to a significant increase in the price of oil.

RENÉ LÉVESQUE AND QUEBEC	CANADA AND THE WORLD

RENÉ LÉVESQUE AND QUEBEC

CANADA AND THE WORLD

In Chile General Pinochet leads a bloody coup, killing President Allende and overthrowing his socialist government.

1974

The sovereigntist daily newspaper *Le Jour* is founded.

Bill 22 proclaims French the official language of Quebec.

The proposal by Claude Morin, the father of gradualism, to achieve independence by means of a referendum is adopted at the Parti Québécois convention.

Michèle Lalonde publishes her poem *Speak White* and Michel Brault directs the film *Les ordres*.

1974

In Canada, the Liberal Party is re-elected.

In the U.S., President Richard Nixon is forced to resign and is succeeded by Vice-President Gerald Ford.

In Greece, the Regime of the Colonels ends and democracy is restored.

1975

Public hearings are held at the Commission of Inquiry on Organized Crime (CIOC).

An agreement is reached with the Cree and Inuit regarding territories in the James Bay area. Their rights to occupy part of the territory are recognized and financial compensation is planned.

1975

In Spain, Franco dies; Juan Carlos becomes King.

In Vietnam, the army of the South surrenders to Communists from the North.

The Khmer Rouge Communist guerrillas, led by Pol Pot, take power in Cambodia and proclaim the Democratic Republic of Kampuchea.

Civil war begins between Muslims and Phalangists in Lebanon.

René Lévesque

RENÉ LÉVESQUE AND QUEBEC

1976
A confrontation occurs between the Association des Gens de l'air, who demand the francization of air space, and English-speaking air controllers.

On November 15, the Parti Québécois is brought to power and René Lévesque becomes premier of Québec.

The Olympic Games are held in Montreal.

1977
Lévesque is named Grand Officer of the Légion d'honneur of France and receives the Médaille de la Ville de Paris.

Bill 101, the Charter of the French Language, is passed.

Legislation on the financing of political parties is passed.

1978
An angry outcry follows the announcement that the head office of the Sun Life Insurance Company is moving to Toronto due to the Charter of the French Language.

1979
René Lévesque marries Corinne Côté. His mother, Diane Dionne, dies.

CANADA AND THE WORLD

1976
Democrat Jimmy Carter is elected president of the U.S.

Vietnam is reunified.

1977
In the U.S.S.R., Leonid Brezhnev is elected chairman of the Presidium of the Supreme Soviet.

1978
In Italy, Aldo Moro, leader of the Christian Democratic Party, is assassinated by the Red Brigades, a terrorist group.

At the Vatican, Jean-Paul II is elected Pope.

1979
Conservative Joe Clark is elected prime minister of Canada.

RENÉ LÉVESQUE AND QUEBEC

The Supreme Court of Canada declares certain articles in the Charter of the French Language unconstitutional.

The LG-2 James Bay power plant is commissioned.

The Youth Protection Act and the Act Respecting Occupational Health and Safety are passed.

1980
A referendum is held May 20 on the PQ government's sovereignty-association project. The turnout rate is 86 per cent and the "no" wins with 60 per cent of the vote.

1981
René Lévesque and the Parti Québécois are re-elected to the National Assembly. They obtain eighty seats (49.2 per cent of the vote) while the Liberal Party obtains forty-two (46 per cent).

1982
Bill 65 is passed, giving access to documents held by public bodies and protecting personal information.

CANADA AND THE WORLD

In the U.S., the Camp David Accord between Egypt and Israel is signed.

In Cambodia, Pol Pot's dictatorship comes to an end.

In Iran, the Shah is overthrown and a new Islamic Republic is established.

1980
Pierre Elliott Trudeau and the Liberal Party win the Canadian federal election.

Republican Ronald Reagan, a former actor, is elected president of the U.S.

In Poland, Solidarity, a free union, is founded. Lech Walesa is elected president the following year.

1981
The federal government patriates the Canadian Constitution without the consent of Quebec.

François Mitterrand, first secretary of the Socialist Party, is elected president of France.

1982
The British North America Act, patriated from London and renamed the Constitution Act, is signed by the Queen and serves as the Canadian Constitution.

RENÉ LÉVESQUE AND QUEBEC

CANADA AND THE WORLD

In the U.S.S.R., Brezhnev dies and Yuri Andropov is appointed first secretary of the Communist Party.

1983
Robert Bourassa again becomes leader of the Liberal Party.

1983
In the U.S., the first test flight of the space shuttle Columbia takes place.

1984
Following a letter to his party's national executive wherein Lévesque claims that sovereignty will not be an issue in the next election, seven ministers leave the cabinet.

1984
John Turner succeeds Pierre Elliott Trudeau as leader of the Liberal Party and as prime minister of Canada. In the election that follows in September, Brian Mulroney's Conservatives defeat the Liberals.

1985
René Lévesque resigns both as premier and as president of the Parti Québécois. Pierre Marc Johnson succeeds him.

Robert Bourassa's Liberal Party wins with ninety-nine seats (55 per cent of the vote). The Parti Québécois wins twenty-three seats (38.6 per cent).

1985
In the U.S.S.R., Mikhail Gorbachev becomes General Secretary of the Communist party. He meets U.S. President Ronald Reagan in order to accelerate U.S.-Soviet dialogue.

1986
René Lévesque publishes his memoirs, *Attendez que je me rappelle*; an English translation by Philip Stratford is also released, under the title *Memoirs*.

1986
At Chernobyl, in the U.S.S.R., the world's most serious nuclear power plant accident to date occurs.

1987
As of August, René Lévesque is a commentator on the program *Point de vue sur l'actualité* on

1987
In Canada, the Meech Lake Accord is signed. It is an agreement in principle between the ten provincial premiers and their fed-

Montreal radio station CKAC. He dies on November 1.

The Meech Lake Accord proposes to recognize Quebec as a distinct society and grant it the right to veto constitutional amendments.

1988
The Supreme Court of Canada declares that Quebec cannot forbid signs in English.

1989
The Liberal Party, led by Robert Bourassa, is re-elected with ninety-two members (49.9 per cent of the vote). The Parti Québécois elects twenty-nine members (40.1 per cent).

1990
The Bélanger-Campeau Commission looks into Quebec's political future.

The events of the Oka Crisis mark the "réveil autochtone," or awakening of First Nations. The Canadian army is called in to demolish the barricades that block the road to Oka and the Mercier Bridge.

1991
Following the failure of Meech Lake, the Allaire Report recom-

eral counterpart on the conditions set out by Quebec to sign the constitutional law of 1982.

1988
Canada signs a commercial free trade agreement with the United States.

In France, President François Mitterrand is re-elected.

1989
Eastern European countries overwhelmingly leave the Communist regime in favour of democracy. In Germany, the Berlin Wall, built in 1961, falls on November 9.

1990
In Canada, the Meech Lake Accord dies when Manitoba and Newfoundland refuse to ratify it, which leads to the founding of the Bloc Québécois, a sovereigntist party on the federal scene.

In Russia, Boris Yeltsin is elected president of the Russian Federation.

The two Germanys reunify.

1991
The Gulf War erupts: after forty days of fighting, Iraq surrenders to

RENÉ LÉVESQUE AND QUEBEC

mends a significant transfer of power from Ottawa to Quebec City.

1992
Premier Robert Bourassa supports the Charlottetown Accord, a proposed constitutional amendment agreed to by federal and provincial leaders meeting in Charlottetown.

1993
Daniel Johnson, son of the Union Nationale former leader, succeeds Robert Bourassa as leader of the Liberal Party.

1994
The Parti Québécois, led by Jacques Parizeau, wins the election.

1995
A second referendum is held on the PQ government's sovereignty-association bill. The "no" vote wins with 50.6 per cent of the vote. Jacques Parizeau leaves politics and is replaced by Lucien Bouchard.

CANADA AND THE WORLD

the forces of the United States and its allies.

In Russia, Yeltsin is elected prime minister by universal vote.

1992
The people of six Canadian provinces, including Quebec, reject the national referendum on the Charlottetown Accord.

1993
Canada's Kim Campbell of the Conservative Party is the first woman to serve as prime minister, but her term is short; in the election, Jean Chrétien's Liberal Party is victorious.

1994
In South Africa, Nelson Mandela becomes the country's first black president.

1995
In Canada, following the results of the Quebec Referendum, the federal government passes a motion to recognize Quebec as a distinct society.

Bibliography

Books

BENJAMIN, Jacques. *Comment on fabrique un premier ministre québécois, de 1960 à nos jours.* Montreal: L'Aurore, 1975.

BERGERON, Gérard. *Notre miroir à deux faces: Trudeau-Lévesque.* Montreal: Québec Amérique, 1985.

DESBARATS, Peter. *René Lévesque ou le projet inachevé.* Trans. by Robert Guy Scully. Montreal: Fides, 1977.

————. *René: A Canadian in Search of a Country.* Toronto: McClelland & Stewart, 1976.

DUCHESNE, Pierre. *Jacques Parizeau, (1970-1985), tome II, Le Baron.* Montreal: Québec Amérique, 2002.

DUPONT, Pierre. *15 novembre 1976...* Montreal: Quinze, 1976.

FOURNIER, Claude. *René Lévesque: Portrait of a Man Alone.* Trans. by Jean-Pierre Fournier. Toronto: McClelland & Stewart, 1995.

FRASER, Graham. *René Lévesque & the Parti Québécois in Power.* Toronto: McClelland & Stewart, 1984.

GODIN, Pierre. *René Lévesque, Un enfant du siècle (1922-1960).* Montreal: Boréal, 1994.

————. *René Lévesque, Héros malgré lui (1960-1976)*. Montreal: Boréal, 1997.

————. *René Lévesque, L'espoir et le chagrin (1976-1980)*. Montreal: Boréal, 2001.

LÉVESQUE, René. *Attendez que je me rappelle*. Montreal: Québec Amérique, 1986.

————. *Memoirs*. Trans. by Philip Stratford. Toronto: McClelland & Stewart, 1986.

————. *Chroniques de René Lévesque*. Montreal: Québec Amérique, 1987.

————. *Option Québec, précédé d'un essai d'André Bernard*. Montreal: Typo, 1997.

————. *An Option for Quebec*. Toronto: McClelland & Stewart, 1968.

MONIÈRE, Denis. *Le développement des idéologies au Québec*. Montreal: Québec Amérique, 1977.

MORIN, Claude. *Lendemains piégés, Du référendum à la nuit des longs couteaux*. Montreal: Boréal, 1988.

————. *Mes premiers ministres: Lesage, Johnson, Bertrand, Bourassa et Lévesque*. Montreal: Boréal, 1991.

PAYETTE, Lise. *Le pouvoir? Connais pas!* Montreal: Québec Amérique, 1982.

PELLETIER, Gérard. *Le temps des choix, 1960-1968*. Montreal: Stanké, 1986, 384 p.

————. *Years of Choice, 1960-1968*. Trans. by Alan Brown. Toronto: Methuen, 1987.

PROVENCHER, Jean. *René Lévesque. Portrait d'un Québécois*. Montreal: La Presse, 1973.

————. *René Lévesque: Portrait of a Québécois*. Trans. by David Ellis. Toronto: Gage, 1975.

VASTEL, Michel. *Landry, le grand dérangeant.* Montreal: Éditions de l'Homme, 2001.

Websites
http://www.vigile.net/ds-histoire/index/levesque.html
http://www.assnat.qc.ca/fra/membres/notices/j-l/lever.htm
http://www.agora.qc.ca/mot.nsf/Dossiers/Rene_Levesque
http://www.partiquebecois.org.zones/www/index.php?
    pg=19
http://www.uottawa.ca/constitutional-law/language1.
    html
http://www.canadahistory.com/sections/papers/papersp
    aquin.htm
http://www.uni.ca/lowe.html http://www2.marianopo-
    lis.edu/quebechistory/readings/ccf-ndp.htm
http://www.pco-bcp.gc.ca/aia/default.asp?Language
    =E&Page=consfile&Sub=ReferendaQuestionsand
    Res
http://collections.ic.gc.ca/SaskIndian/a82may10.htm
http://english.republiquelibre.org/studies.html
http://en.wikipedia.org/wiki/October_Crisis
http://encyclopedia.thefreedictionary.com/Timeline%2
    0of%20Quebec%20history

Recording
Bouchard, Jacques. *Point de mire sur René Lévesque.*
    Montreal: Radio-Canada/GSI Musique, box of 11
    compact discs and booklet.

Films
CYR, Luc et Carl LEBLANC. *Canada by Night.* Montreal: Ad
    Hoc films, "24 heures pour l'Histoire," series, 1999.

LABRECQUE, Jean-Claude. *Le RIN — Rassemblement pour l'indépendance nationale*. Montreal: Productions Virage et Télé-Québec, 2002.
SPRY, Robin. *The October Crisis of 1970*. N.F.B., 1973, 87 minutes.

Index

Page numbers in *italics* indicate photographs.

12th Army Group, 41

L'Action catholique, 35, 131
Action libérale nationale, 33, 127
Les Actualités canadiennes, 48, 131
Agence France-Presse, 83
agricultural zoning legislation, 18
Algeria, 55, 134
Alma, Quebec, 9
American army, 37, 38, 41, 131
American Broadcasting Station, 40
anglophone community of Quebec, 13
anti-scab legislation, 18
Article I of PQ, 93
Asbestos strike, 51, 60, 132
Assimopoulos, Nadia, 122
Attendez que je me rappelle.
    See Memoirs
Au lendemain de la veille
    (TV program), 135
automobile insurance legislation, 18, 21
autonomy. *See* Quebec:
    sovereignty
Les Aventures de Max Fuchs
    (TV program), 134

Baie des Chaleurs, 26, 29, 31
Barbados, 120
Barre, Madame Raymond, 25
Barrette, Antonio, 60, 135
Baulu, Roger, 47
Bédard, Marc-André, 22, 24, 121
Bertrand, François, 47
Bertrand, Jean-Jacques, 81, 139

Bill 22, 141
Bill 63, 81, 139
Bill 101, 13, 16-18, 100, 121, 142
Bissonnette, Lise, 107
Bloc Québécois, 145
Bonaventure County, Gaspé, 27
Borduas, Paul-Émile, 50, 132
Bouchard, Lucien, 118, 146
Bourassa, Robert, 5-7, 11, 22, 82-
    84, 86, 87, 95, 98, 117, 123, 140,
    144, 145, 146
Bourgault, Pierre, 79, 80, 93, 94,
    137
Bradley, General Omar, 41
Brière, Marc, 85
British North America Act, 143
British Parliament, 111
Burns, Robert, 101
"the bunker," 7, 16, 23, 24, 101,
    102

cabinet of PQ government, 1, 5-8,
    16, 21-24, 101, 102, 118-120, 144
cabinet of Quebec Liberal Party
    government, 60, 61, 64, 66, 70
Caisse de dépôt et placement du
    Québec, 71, 138
Cambodia, 24, 141, 143
Canada, 17, 32, 69, 75, 76, 101,
    102, 104, 111, 125-133, 135-146
Canadian army, 39, *74*, 88, 130,
    145
Canadian Battalion (UN), 51
Canadian Broadcasting
    Corporation, 57, 127, 129
Canadian Confederation, 3, 69, 76,
    118
Canadian Constitution. *See*
    Constitution

Canadian Press, 101
Carrefour (TV program), 54, 134
CBFT (TV station), 133
Cercle des journalistes de
    Montréal, *46*
Charbonneau, Msgr. Joseph, 129,
    132, 133
Charlottetown Accord, 146
Charron, Claude, 5, 6, 116
Charter of the French Language.
    See Bill 101
Charter of Rights and Freedoms,
    111
CHNC (radio station), 128
Choquette, Jérôme, 85
Choquette, Robert, 48
Chrétien, Jean, *124*, 146
CKAC (radio station), 88, 98, 122
CKCV (radio station), 129
Clark, Joe, 25, 102, 142
Collège Saint-Charles-Garnier, *28*,
    34-36, 37, 128, 129
Colombey-les-Deux-Églises,
    France, 18-20
Confederation of National Trade
    Unions (CNTU/CSN), 125
Conférence de presse (TV
    program), 134
Conservative Party of Canada, 25,
    102, 118, 126, 135, 142, 144, 146
Conservative Party of Quebec,
    126, 127
Constitution, Canadian, 3, 108;
    negotiations, 108, 109, 110, 112,
    116, 117, 140, 143-145
Constitutional law of 1982, 145
consumer protection legislation, 18
Côté, Corinne (second wife), 1, 9,
    10, 15, 21, 25, 81, 112, 120, 142
Cross, James Richard, 83-85, 87,
    88, 89, 90, 139
Crown corporations, 64

Dachau, Germany, 42-44, 49, 130-
    131
Derome, Bernard, 99
Le Devoir, 5, 75, 87, 107, 118
Dieppe, 37, 130
Dimanche-Matin, 138
Dionne, Diane (mother), 26, 27,
    29, 37, 40, 41, 47, 126, 128, 129;
    death, 26, 142; hopes for R.L. to
    become a lawyer, 31, 36
distinct society, 145, 146
Dorion riding, 96, 140
Dorval·riding, 53
Duplessis, Maurice, 21, 32, 41, 47,
    50, 51, 61, 63, 64, 127, 128, 130,
    132-135; death, 60, 135

Eastern Townships, Quebec, 5
Eaton's (store), 17, 116, 139
École des hautes études
    commerciales, 82
Economic Club, 11, 12
Égalité ou indépendance (by
    Daniel Johnson), 71
Elizabeth, Princess/Queen, 53,
    117, 133, 135, 137, 143
employee stock savings plan, 18
Enfant-Jésus Hospital, Quebec
    City, 120
Expo 67: 19, 138

family allowances, 71
federal elections, 25, 78, 79, 117,
    125-127, 130, 132, 135, 139,
    140-144, 146
federal-provincial relations, 8, 9,
    108-112, 117, 128, 134, 140, 143
Ferré, Léo, 89
Ferron, Jacques, 31
Fort Prével, Quebec, 118
France, 18-21, 25, 36, 41, 48, 127-
    130, 135, 143, 145
Free French Forces, 42, 129

free trade with U.S., 122, 145
French army, 36
French-English inequality in
   Quebec, 29, 64, 68, 69
Front de libération du Québec
   (FLQ), 69, 83-85, 87, 90, 114,
   137, 139; manifesto of, 84, 85

"the Gang of Eight," 110
Garon, Jean, 6
Gaspé, 10, 32, 34, 115, 118, 127
de Gaulle, Charles, 18-20, 75, 129,
   135, 138, 140
Gauvreau, Claude, 50
Germany and Germans, 36, 37, 39,
   40, 42-45, 127-130, 132, 133,
   136, 145
Gestapo, 43, 44
Giguère, Roland, 80
Giscard d'Estaing, Valérie, 20-21
Godbout, Adelard, 127-130
gradualism, 3, 5, 141
Great Britain, 36, 38, 40, 128, 129,
   131, 133
Grégoire, Gilles, 80
Groulx, Lionel, 33
Guilbault, Muriel, 50
Guimond, Olivier, 59

health insurance legislation, 70,
   130, 135, 140
Hiroshima, 47, 131
House of Commons, 73, 102, 105
Hull, Quebec, 109
Hungary, 54, 134
Hydro-Québec, 66, 119, 130-131,
   136, 137

immigrants in Quebec, 81, 82
Indochinois (ship), 39
Les interviews de René Lévesque
   (radio program), 132
Inuit art, 56

Iran, 24, 143
Italy, 26, 45, 126, 129-130, 142

Jasmin, Judith, 48, 50, 53, 54, 131,
   134
Johnson, Daniel (Union Nationale
   leader), 68, 71, 138; death, 81,
   139
Johnson, Daniel (Quebec Liberal
   Party leader), 146
Johnson, Pierre Marc, 118, 122,
   144
Le Jour, 97, 98, 141
Journal de Montréal, 85, 88, 90,
   97, 140
Journal de Québec, 140
Journalistes au micro (radio
   program), 132

Kelly, John Hall, 27
Kennedy, John F., 68, 135, 137
Khrushchev, Nikita, 61, 134, 137
Kierans, Eric, 70
King, Mackenzie, 32, 50, 125, 127,
   130
Korean War, 46, 50-52, 132-134

labour unions. *See* unions in
   Quebec
Lac Achigan, 85
Lac à l'Épaule, 66
Lagacé, Lorraine, 116
language legislation. *See* Bill 22;
   Bill 63; Bill 101
Lapalme, Georges-Émile, 67, 133
Laporte, Pierre, 85-90, 139;
   murder, 26, 88, 139
Larocque, André, 93
Lasalle, Roch, 110
Laurendeau, André, 126
Laurendeau-Dunton Commission.
   See Royal Commission on
   Bilingualism and Biculturalism

Laurier, Sir Wilfrid, 32, 95
Laurin, Camille, xi, 16-18, 23, 120, 121
Laval University. *See* Université Laval
Lebrun, Roland, 36
Lecavalier, René, 47
Leclerc, Félix, 123
Le May, Pamphile, 118
Lesage, Jean, 56, 57, 60, 61, 63, 64, 66-68, 70, 71, 75, 76, 86, 135
Lévesque, Alice (sister), 33, 40
Lévesque, André (brother), 33, 40
Lévesque, Claude (son), 132
Lévesque, Dominique (father), 27, 29-31, 33, 36, 126, 128; death, 34, 128
Lévesque, Fernand (brother), 33, 40
Lévesque, Pierre (son), 49, 132
Lévesque, René
  admires the U.S., 10-12, 39
  automobile accident, 15, 16
  bilingual, 16, 31, 39
  birth and childhood, 10, 26, 27, 28, 29-31, 126
  bohemian, 36
  "butcher of New Carlisle," 115
  charisma, radio and TV style, 23, 52, 54, 55, 61, 62, 68, 96
  death, 122, 144
  democratic ideals, 2-4, 44, 84, 103
  disillusionment, 112, 118
  education, 28, 31, 32, 34, 35-37, 127-129
  election candidate, 60-63, 67, 68, 71, 89, 90, 92, 93, 94, 95, 98, 99, 109, 116, 136, 138, 140, 142, 143
  enters politics, 61, 121, 136
  epitaph, 122
  federalist views, 69

  feeling of exile in English Canada, 34, 69, 75
  first jobs in radio, 33, 128, 129
  first marriage, 49, 131
  founds Mouvement sou-veraineté-association, 4, 138
  friendships, relations with colleagues, 22, 35, 48, 65, 75, 119, 121
  gambler, 25, 29, 30, 104, 117, 118
  grandparents, 29, 30
  hardworking, 22, 24, 49
  honours received, 20, 142
  incorruptible, 8, 62-64
  independent MNA, 80, 138
  interest in international politics, 24, 47, 49
  interest in journalism, 34, 44, 48, 49, 122
  journalist, 18, 24, 73; CKAC (radio), 121, 144; international service (Radio-Canada), 48-50, 131-134; *Journal de Montréal*, 85, 88, 90, 97, 140; national radio (Radio-Canada), 53, 130-133; Télé-Métropole, 122; television, 11, 54, 55, 58-60, 61, 68, 97, 134, 135; war correspondent, 37, 38, 43, 44, 46, 51, 52, 55, 130, 133
  leader of PQ, 91, 92, 115, 116
  legislation on financing political parties, 4, 100, 142
  love of reading, history, 30, 32
  memoirs, 122, 144, 148
  minister in Lesage government, 56, 63-71, 136, 137
  moderate views, 4, 6, 13, 16, 17, 23, 26, 44, 78, 79, 80, 82, 84, 94
  moderating influence, 8, 93, 94, 97, 100
  modesty, 20

nationalizes resources, electrical power, 21, 65-68, 136, 137

opposition MNA, 72, 75-77, 90, 93, 95

poker player, 24, 25, 29, 30, 35, 36, 40, 41, 51, 93, 110

premier of Quebec, 2-11, 15-22, 99, 142-144

reaction to Pierre Laporte's murder, 26, 85, 86, 88

reforms made as Minister of Family and Social Services, 70, 71

relations with women, 9, 10, 15, 22, 24, 41, 48, 53, 58, 81, 97, 112, 113

relationship with young family, 49, 51, 52, 55, 58

resigns as leader of PQ, 122, 144

resigns from Liberal Party, 9, 77, 121, 138

resilient, tenacious, 105, 106, 114, 121

second marriage, 24, 25, 142

smoking and alcohol consumption, 12, 16, 17, 21, 24, 25, 35, 36, 40, 61, 66, 75, 99, 102, 116, 117, 119

sovereigntist position, 9, 13, 15, 73, 74-77, 79, 82, 100, 103, 117-119, 122

and strike at Radio-Canada, 57-60, 135

tennis player, 32, 48, 85

viewed as communist, 61

viewed as nationalist, 71

voice quality, 42, 47, 52, 53, 63, 106

willful, demanding, 6, 22, 97

writer (apart from journalism), 2, 11, 12, 35, 116, 122, 129, 144, 148

Lévesque, Suzanne (daughter), 134

L'Heureux, Louise (first wife), 10, 35, 40, 48, 49, 51, 52, 58, 97, 131

Liberal Party of Canada, 50, 78, 79, 94, 127, 132, 138, 140, 141, 143, 144, 146. *See also* federal elections

Liberal Party of Quebec. *See* Quebec Liberal Party

lieutenant-governor of Quebec, 116

linguistic rights, 81, 82, 139, 140, 143. *See also* Bill 63; Bill 101

London, England, 40, 41, 126, 130, 143

Longueuil, Quebec, *xiv, 14*

Lorraine, France, 19, 20

MacArthur, General Douglas, 50, 133

Maîtres chez nous slogan, 33, 68, 136

Manic dams (Manicouagan River), 81, 138

Manitoba, 145

Marceau family, 35

Marchand, Jean, 51, 60, 61, 73

Marler, Georges, 67

Maurice Richard Arena, 78

Meech Lake Accord, 144, 145

Memoirs (Attendez que je me rappelle), 122, 144, 148

Michaud, Yves, 120

Mi'Kmaq people, 32

Milan, Italy, 45

Le Monde, 24

Montreal, 2, 16, 17, 19, 47-49, 53, 55, 57, 59, 60, 66, 72, 74, 75, 77, 81, 83, 87, 88, 90, 95, 113, 116, 120, 122, 123, 126, 131, 138, 139, 140, 142

Montreal-Laurier riding, 61-63, 76, 77, 82, 121, 136, 138, 140
Montreal North, 90
Montreal Olympics, 6, 8, 142
Montreal Standard, 30
Morin, Claude, 3, 5, 12, 23, 93, 94, 103, 110, 116, 117, *124*, 141
Morin, Jacques-Yvan, 5
Morrow, Joseph, 54
Moscow, 62
Mouvement souveraineté-association (MSA). *See* Sovereignty-Association Movement (MSA)
Mulroney, Brian, 118, 144
Mussolini, Benito, 45, 126

Nagasaki, 47, 131
Nasser, Abdel Gamal, 54
National Assembly (Quebec), 3, 17, 24, 81, 85, 86, 88, 93-97, 99, 100, 103, 105, 109, 120, 121, 143
nationalization of electric power. *See* Lévesque, René: nationalizes resources, electrical power. *See also*, Hydro-Quebec
Nazis, 42, 128
New Carlisle, Quebec, 16, 26, 29, 30, 33, 34, 115, 126, 128
New Deal, 10
Newfoundland, 126, 132, 145
New Jersey, 11
New York City, 11, 66
New York Times, 24
"Night of the Long Knives," 112, 119
Nixon, Richard, 68, 139, 140, 141
Noranda Mines, 64
Normandy, France, 37, 130
La nouvelle entente Québec-Canada (PQ white paper), 103

occupational health and safety legislation, 18
October Crisis, 82-89, 90, 91, 139
Office of War Information, 39, 130
Ontario, 13
opting out (constitutional provision), 110, 112
Option Québec, 9, 10, 78, 139, 148
Ottawa, 8, 9, 20, 25, 50, 59, 70, 71, 73-75, 76, 78, 84, 85, 95, 101, 110, 111, 118, *124*, 145

Parizeau, Jacques, 5, 6, 65, 66, 82, 93, 103-105, 110, 115, 122, 139, 146
Parti Créditiste, 96
Parti Québécois, 2, 3, 6, 11, 17, 18, 22, 23, 25, 80, 82, 85, 87, 89, 91, 93, 122, 139, 140; conventions, 3, 6, 91-94, 96, 100, 102, 112, 114, 115, 117, 118, 119, 120, 140-143; divisions in, 3, 23, 93-95, 101, 103, 110, 114, 117-120, 144; elections, 4, 5, 8, 9, 82-83, 92, 94, 95, 97, 98-99, 108, 109, 111, 112, 116, 120, 140, 142, 144, 146; reforms during first mandate, 18, 143
Paspébiac Point, 31
Patton, General, 41, 42, 130
Paul Sauvé Centre, 1-2, 83, 92, 96, 99, 100, 106, 109
Payette, Lise, 1, 6, 7, 21, 22, 107, 109
Pearson, Lester B., 69, 78, 134-137
Pelletier, Albert (stepfather), 26, 34, 128, 129
Pelletier, Denise, 59
Pelletier, Gérard, 60, 61, 73, 133
Le Petit Journal, 133
Philip, Prince, 53, 133
Point de mire (TV progam), 11, 54, 55, 58-60, 62, 68, 134, 135

Point de vue sur l'actualité (radio program), 122, 144
political party financing legislation, 4, 6, 18, 21, 62, 63, 100, 142
Pour un Québec souverain dans une nouvelle union canadienne (article), 75
Premier plan (TV program), 135
La Presse, 126
press conferences, *xiv*, 24, 87
Princesse à marier (play), 129
Proulx, Jacques, 122

Quebec: economy, 65, 66, 68, 115; flag, 49; natural resources, 64, 66; relations with France, 20; social climate, 22, 41, 47, 50, 54, 70, 81; sovereignty, 3, 4, 93-98, 100-113, 116, 117, 121, 138, 141, 143, 144
Quebec City, 7, 13, *28*, 33-36, 40, 45, 48, 49, 63, 66, 74, 80, 93, 96, *108*, 110, 112, 116, 120, 128, 137, 145
Quebec Federation of Labour (QFL/FTQ), 135
Quebec Liberal Party, 6, 8, 9, 22, 23, 60-63, 65, 67-71, 73-76, 80-82, 85, 86, 88, 89, 93, 94, 97, 98, 104, 116, 120, 122, 125-131, 133, 135-140, 143-146; 1967 convention, 74-76
Queen Elizabeth. *See* Elizabeth, Princess/Queen
Queen Elizabeth Hotel, 56, 87
Quiet Revolution, 21, 54, 65, 69, 135

Radio-Canada (radio and television), *46*, 47-49, 51-55, 68, 84, 99, 127, 129-134; strike, 57-60, 135

Ralliement national (RN), 73, 80, 139
Rassemblement pour l'indépendance nationale (RIN), 69-70, 73, 78, 79, 136, 137, 139
Referendum of 1980, 2, 3, 35, 103, 104, 105, *108*, 109, 110, 113, 118, 119, 141, 143
Referendum of 1995, 146
referendum plans and strategy, 2, 3, 4, 21-23, 25, 93, 94, 97, 101-106, 111, 114, 118, 119, 121
Reform Club, 98
Refus global, 50, 132
La revue de l'actualité, 133
La Revue des arts et lettres (radio), 133
Rivière-du-Loup, 29, 34
Robb, Phil, 39
Roosevelt, Franklin D., 10, 39, 127, 130, 131
Rougeau, Johnny, 62
Rouyn-Noranda, 64
Royal Canadian Mounted Police (RCMP), 116, 140
Royal Commission on Bilingualism and Biculturalism, 69, 137, 138
Rutebeuf, 89
Ryan, Claude, 87, 105, 107, *108*, 109

Saint-Denis Club, 75
Saint-Jean-Baptiste Day of 1968, 79
Saint-Laurent, Louis, 50, 132
Saint-Léonard, Montreal, 80
Saint-Michel de Sillery cemetery, 123
Sauvé, Paul, 60, 135
Second World War, 19, 36-45, 47, 49, 50, 128-131
Semaine de la Francophonie (1987), 122

Séminaire de Gaspé, 31, 32, 34, 127
Séminaire de Québec, 129
Seoul, Korea, 50
SGF, 64, 136
Shawinigan Power Company, 67
SOQUEM, 64, 137
Sovereignty-Association Movement (MSA), 2, 4, 17, 19, 73, 75, 78, 80, 93, 118-119, 138, 139, 141, 146
Soviet Union. *See* U.S.S.R.
Stalin, Joseph, 47, 126, 134
St. Hubert, Quebec, 90
St. Hubert Airport, 89
St. Lambert, 86
Strasbourg, France, 42
Suez Canal, 54, 134
A Sunday in Korea with the 22nd Regiment, 52
Supreme Court of Canada, 143, 145
Sylvestre, Claude, 55, 58

Taillon riding, 99
Tarte, Israel, 62
Taschereau, Louis-Alexandre, 32, 125-127
Télé-Métropole, 110, 122
television, 53, 54, 68, 127, 133
Théâtre du Gésu, 59
de Tocqueville, Alexis, 12
Toronto, 12, 57, 59, 142
Trois-Rivières, 32
Trottier, Edgar, 15

Trudeau, Pierre Elliott, 8, 9, 25, 61, 73, 78-80, 84, 88, 95, 102, 105, 106, *108*, 109-112, 117, *124*, 133, 139, 140, 143, 144
Truman, Harry, 47, 49, 50, 131
Turner, John, 144

Union des artistes, 59
Union Nationale, 33, 47, 60, 61, 62, 68, 71, 72, 81-83, 96, 110, 132-135, 138, 146
unions in Quebec, 22, 24, 94, 125, 135; relations with PQ, 23, 102, 115
United Nations (UN),50, 51, 131, 132, 134
United States (U.S.), 10, 19, 39, 49, 64, 66, 122, 125, 127, 129, 131, 133, 135-145
Université Laval, 9, 36, 129
U.S.S.R., 26, 54, 126, 129, 131, 134-138, 142-144

Valcartier, Quebec, 36
Victoria Conference (1971), 140
Vietnam, 24, 126, 131, 134, 136, 137, 140, 141, 142
Vigneault, Gilles, 1, 2
Villeneuve, Cardinal, 35

War Measures Act, *74*, 88, 90, 139
Westmount, Quebec, 69, 83

Yalta Conference, 47
"Yvette" episode, 107, 109

Printed in October 2004
at Imprimerie Gauvin,
Gatineau (Québec).